PHARMACEUTICAL PACKAGING INNOVATIONS

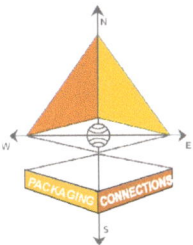

Sanex Packaging Connections Pvt. Ltd.
www.packagingconnections.com

Copyright

Published by :

Sanex Packaging Connections Pvt. Ltd.

An ISO 9001 : 2008 Certified Organisation

117, Suncity Tower, Sector-54

Golf Course Road, Gurgoan-122 002.

Tel : +91 124 4965770

Fax : + 91 124 41433951

e-mail : info@packagingconnections.com

Like us on Facebook : www.facebook.com/pconnection

ISBN : 978-9385010002

PHARMACEUTICAL PACKAGING INNOVATIONS

List of Contributors

Team www.PackagingConnections.com by Sanex Packaging Connections Pvt Ltd

Sandeep Kumar Goyal, Founder & CEO
Amita Venkatesh Valleesha, Associate: Scientific Affairs & Consultancy
Chhavi Goel, Associate: Research & Business Consulting
Bhaskar Ch, Technology Advisor e-business
Radhika Rewri: Executive Technical
Kuldeep Karan, Graphics/Web Designer

PHARMACEUTICAL PACKAGING INNOVATIONS

Table of Contents

PHARMACEUTICAL PACKAGING INNOVATIONS

Introduction

Idea behind this book is to bring the innovations to wider group of professionals to meet the mission of packaging knowledge sharing and that too cost effectively. We feel that this publication will further fill the project pipelines of companies and improve the standards of packaging. Many professionals either do not have the access or time to go through so many innovations together. So we think this publication will fill that gap. For your feedback please email directly to info@packagingconnections.com

With this, Enjoy Wonders Of Packaging!

Sandeep Kumar Goyal
Founder & CEO ,
www.PackagingConnections.com

Pharmaceutical Packaging

Packaging is not a recent phenomenon. It is an activity closely associated with the evolution of society and, as such, can be tracked back to human beginnings. The nature, degree, and amount of Packaging at any stage of society's growth reflect the needs, cultural patterns, material availability, and technology of that society. The pace of the technological change in Packaging field is bringing new innovative packaging ideas and Pharmaceutical Packaging is not an exception.

Society is changing daily; meeting new challenge, integrating new knowledge, accommodating new needs. These changes are inevitably reflected in the way we package, deliver and consume goods. Pharmaceutical Packaging though a concept started from the evolution of civilization, meeting new challenges everyday making it necessary to keep innovating.

History of Pharmaceutical Packaging

Pharmaceutical Packaging is much specialised field. It is quite broad, encompassing, and multi-faceted task and quite challenging as it requires the application of a large amount of scientific and engineering expertise. Historically, packaging of pharmaceutical products has been done in two forms. One is unit dose packing and the second is multi dose packing.

The most significant advance in the packaging of drugs used in hospitals was the introduction of the unit doses for oral medicines. Although strip packaging for an aspirin-based product (Aspro) started in 1927, some 20 years elapsed before the concept was widely used. During the early 1950s, some tablets and capsules were available packages individually into pockets in a continuous tube, and capsules were available packaged individually unto pockets in a continuous tube, the pockets being separated from each other by perforation in the foil strip. From this concept, the hospital unit dose evolved. The advantages are obvious: this form of packaging controls the dispensing and administering of a prescribed single dose of the correct drug at the right time, and it significantly reduced hospital errors, especially when prefilled disposable syringes came in use in the USA in the 1960s.

Blister packaging, first introduced in American hospitals, was an even greater improvement in safe dispensing. The tablet or capsule is visible through the 'blister' and the product can thus be recognised before the package is opened. Today both strip packs and blister packs are used world widely.

Global Pharmaceutical Packaging Market:

Refer to a research document published by Transparency Market Research, titled "Global and U.S. Pharmaceutical Packaging - Industry Analysis, Size, Share, Growth, Trends and Forecast, 2012 - 2018". **The global and U.S. pharmaceutical packaging market** was worth US$50.07 billion in 2011. It is expected to grow at a CAGR of 5.6% from 2012 to 2018, eventually attaining an overall market value of US$73.04 billion in 2018.

Key participants in the pharmaceutical packaging market include Amcor, Gerresheimer AG, Becton Dickinson, MeadWestvaco, Rexam PLC, West Pharmaceutical Services, 3M and Tear and Tape among others.

The r eport states that the **Asia Pacific region** is expected to show an increase in demand in the global pharmaceutical packaging market. It stated that North America held the largest market share in 2011. It held more than 30%, due to the huge demand for pharmaceutical packaging in Canada and the U.S. this dominance could soon be cut short by Asia Pacific, which is currently the fastest growing region in the pharmaceutical packaging market. By 2018, the region could effectively hold more than 25% of the market share. The market in Asia Pacific is expected to reach USD 20.63 billion by 2018. Development of innovative packaging that provides a combination of product protection, quality, security, tamper evidence and visual appeal to enhance consumer consumption and reduce counterfeiting and other malpractices is expected to boost the market within the forecast period. Furthermore, implementation of numerous stringent regulations by authorized agencies such as Healthcare

Compliance Packaging Council (HCPC), National Quality Forum (NQF) and Food and Drug Administration (FDA) for pharmaceutical packaging is expected to contribute to the growth of the market over the next few years. Issue of environment safety is also key concern for both developed and developing countries packaging industry.

Packaging Requirement & its Importance:

Packaging is a system which allows containment of pharmaceutical product from the time of production in a unit till its use. Unlike other products, particularly medicinal drugs need more care in their packaging because any failure in their packing could result in reducing the

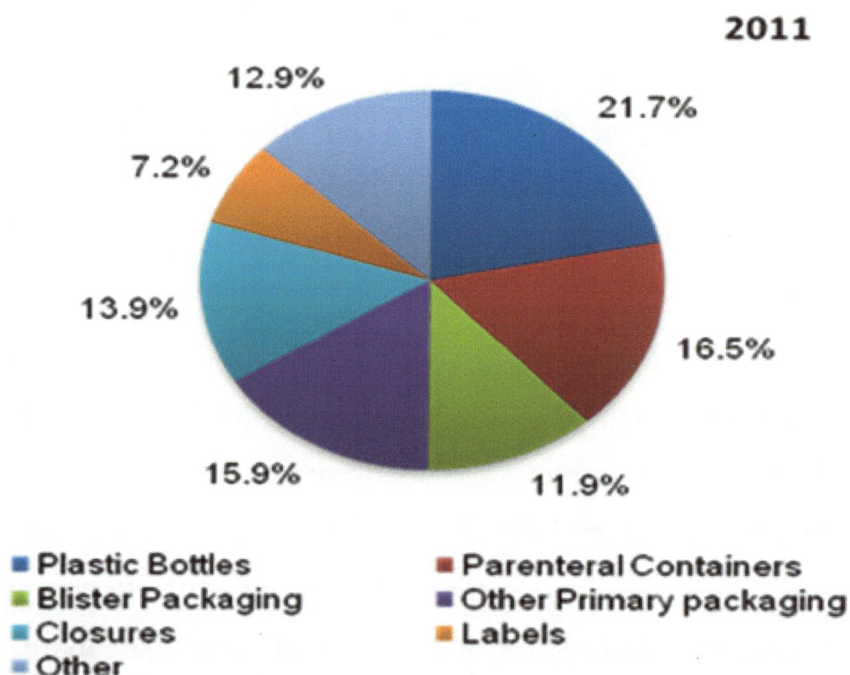

2011

- 12.9%
- 7.2%
- 21.7%
- 13.9%
- 16.5%
- 15.9%
- 11.9%

■ Plastic Bottles   ■ Parenteral Containers
■ Blister Packaging   ■ Other Primary packaging
■ Closures   ■ Labels
■ Other

Global Pharmaceutical Packaging market volume share, by product segment.
[Source: ECA, Pharmaworld magazine, Primary interviews, Transparency Market Research]

efficacy of the drug that may lead either to a failure to cure or even cause death of patient. Role of pharmaceutical packaging is to provide life saving drugs, surgical devices, blood and blood products, nutraceuticals, powders, poultices, liquid and dosage forms, solid and semisolid dosage forms.

Pharmaceutical packaging has to be carried out for the purpose of the safety of the pharmaceutical preparations in order to keep them free from contamination, hinder microbial growth, and ensure product safety through the intended shelf life for the pharmaceuticals. It has to balance lots of complex considerations. Leaving behind relatively simple issues such as developing good designs and communicating with customers, pharmaceutical companies are concerned to more pressing concerns which include fighting with counterfeiting, encouraging patient compliance, ensuring drug integrity and balancing child-resistance and accessibility for the elderly. Packaging is a critical tool in the pharmaceutical industry for product delivery and regulatory compliance, many pharmaceutical companies will do all their packaging within a contamination free environment or Clean room. Packaging of pharmaceuticals essentially provides containment, drug safety, identity, convenience of handling and delivery.

Packaging used for Pharmaceutical:

Packaging of pharmaceutical products begins with the material selection and it drives the choice and type of packaging equipment and final package performance which decides the success of packaging. The packaging material choice drives the pharmaceutical product's appearance and consumer attributes. It determines how a product is manufactured, filled, sterilized, labelled, bundled, distributed, and presented to the customer. It can influence where a customer looks for a package in a retail store, how the customer uses the product at home, and how a hospital, nursing home, or retailer handles a product through their inventory and distribution system.

The primary and secondary packaging of pharmaceutical products is directly associated to their production and constitutes an integral part of the value added process while tertiary packaging related to the logistics such as cold chain. A distinction must be made between primary and secondary packaging vials, closures, blisters) are in direct physical contact with the product, whereas the secondary components are not (e.g. aluminium caps, cardboard boxes). The choice of primary and/or secondary packaging materials will depend on the degree of protection required, compatibility with the contents, the filling method and cost, but also the presentation for over-the-counter (OTC) drugs and the convenience of the packaging for the user (e.g. size, weight, method of opening/ reclosing (if appropriate), legibility of printing).

For manufacturing of primary or secondary there are packaging material used in the pharmaceutical industry: Cardboard (Boxes, Display units' Paper Labels, Leaflets); Glass Ampoules (Bottles, Vials, Syringes, Cartridges); Plastic Closures (Bottles, Bags, Tubes, Laminates with paper or foil); Metal, e.g. aluminium Collapsible tubes (Rigid cans, Foils, Needles; Gas cylinders; Pressurized containers); Rubber (Closures, including plungers) etc.

Need for innovations

Pharmaceutical packaging firms are some of the industry's leading innovators evident by the recent advancement in technology. The current trends are result of continuous series of challenges faced by industry. Packaging is a science which is continuously evolving and is a major success contributor for pharmaceutical industries.

Consumers are demanding for better features and convenience in packaging products. Child-resistant, senior friendly, tamper evident, and anti-counterfeit packaging are in great demand worldwide. Besides, ageing world population, increasing requirement for convenience among consumers, growing requirements for brand differentiation, new packaging material development, increasing awareness of environmental issues, and the adoption of new regulatory requirements are going to be the key growth drivers for future of pharmaceutical packaging business.

Rapidly evolved pharmaceutical industry and an educated consumer have forced Pharmaceutical packaging to undergo paradigm shift in the past few years. The industry has kept itself armed with technological innovations to provide sustainable and affordable packaging solutions. The decision making power and choice of features has empowered the consumers and this has kept the industry on its toes. At the same time, the method in which the drugs are administered have also changed for better dosage control and patient safety. These developments are proving crucial in the growth of pharmaceutical industry. Pharmaceutical packaging can make a huge difference here.

PHARMACEUTICAL PACKAGING INNOVATIONS

INNOVATIONS

PHARMACEUTICAL PACKAGING INNOVATIONS

RESINS AND ADHESIVE

PHARMACEUTICAL PACKAGING INNOVATIONS

Manufacturer/Designer

Clariant Chemicals (India) Limited
P.O. Sandoz Baug Kolshet Road
Thane 400 607
India/Asia
Phone: +91 22 2531 5416
Fax : +91 22 2531 5404
www.clariant.in

• Clariant's innovative color and performance materials MEVOPUR® for medical and pharmaceutical applications range meet the latest industry trends for surface functionality and aesthetics still taking into account safety and regulatory compliance.

• MEVOPUR color and performance additives are developed and produced at ISO 13485 certified facility

Application:

• Product differentiation for device or pharmaceutical packaging through the use of vibrant colors.

• Visualization of surgical devices. Using the different options in radiopaque technology, even thin wall sections can be seen when in the body.

• Surface engineering advantages that help to improve the ease of use and reliability of devices.

• Activation of the polymer for laser marking providing ink or solvent residue-free identification;

• Fluorine-free lubrication systems lowers friction between parts reducing force to rotate, slide and actuate helping the reliability of metered dose devices;

• Permanent antistatic agents help to ensure smooth delivery of powdered drugs;

•Addition of anti-microbial additives helps to reduce the transmission of bacteria and spread of infection;

• Covert and non-covert anti-counterfeit systems can be added to the polymer

PHARMACEUTICAL PACKAGING INNOVATIONS

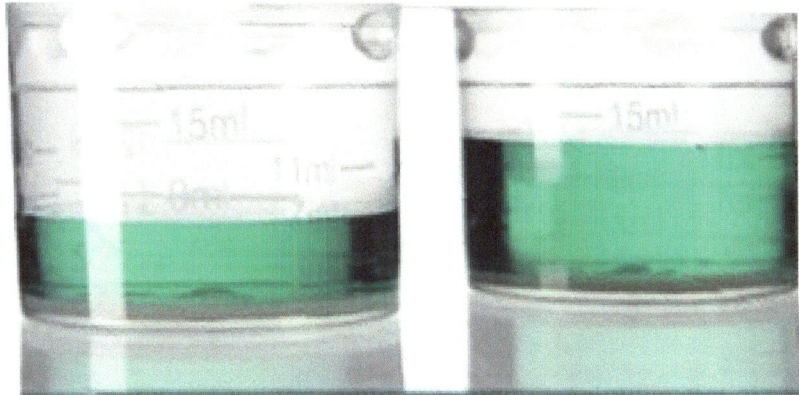

Manufacturer/Designer

Sabic
P.O box 5101
Riyadh11422
Saudi Arabia
Phone: +966 1 225 8000
www.sabic.com

• Sabic's new polypropylene medical grade SABIC® PP PCGR40. in an ultra clear PP liquid medicine dosage delivery system launched by pharmaceutical packaging company Bormioli Rocco.

• The new plastic will be mainly used to produce dosing cups that are more transparent and stronger than previous versions made from various grades of polystyrene and polypropylene, whilst remaining compliant with strict European medical regulations.

• It helps in gain competitive advantage for their core product, such as enhanced transparency and lower conversion costs.

Manufacturer/Designer

UPM RAFLATAC OY
TESOMANKATU 31, P.O. BOX 53,
33310,TAMPERE,PIRKANMAA,
Finland
Tel: +358 20416143
Fax: +358 204168037
communications@upmraflatac.com
www.upmraflatac.com

• Whenever using pressure sensitive labels on LDPE eye-dropper bottles, for example, leachables could migrate through the LDPE and into the liquid– and a need for adhesive with low leachable characteristics.

• RP 31 purus is a low leachable characteristic adhesive

• Excellent mandrel performance

• Environmentally friendly APEO-free (alkyl phenol ethoxylate) formulation, compliant with EU DIRECTIVE 2003/53/EC.

• Approved by FDA and ISEGA, also for blood bag labelling.

• Suitable for sterilization by e-beam- and gamma radiation as well as EtO.

• Upgraded support documentation for Pharmaceutical companies: A new validation support package that will be supplied directly and uniquely to pharmaceutical companies upon request

• Reliability through long-term adhesion

• Migration-safe choice

PHARMACEUTICAL PACKAGING INNOVATIONS

LIDDING AND FLEXIBLE

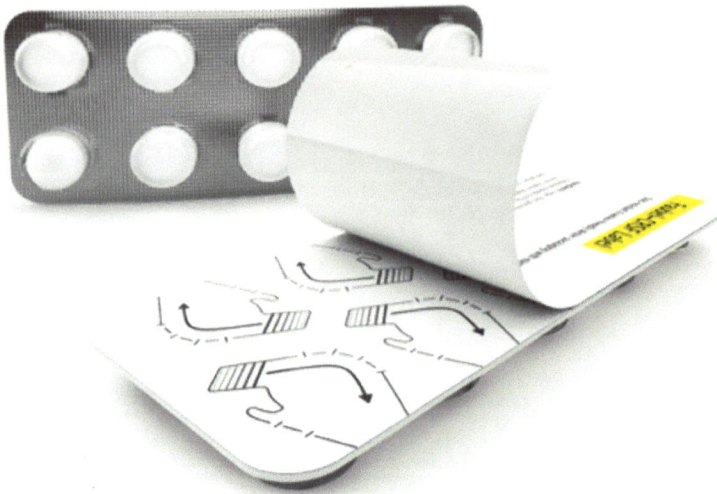

STEP I

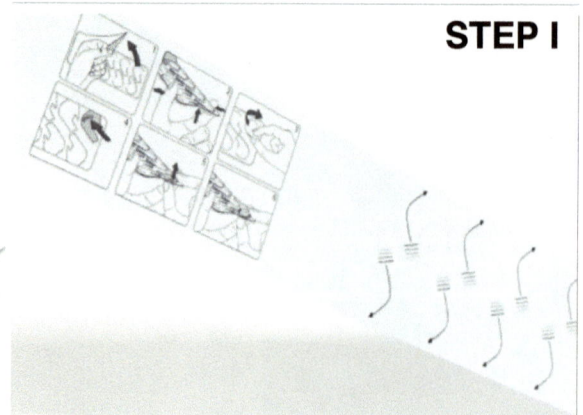

STEP II

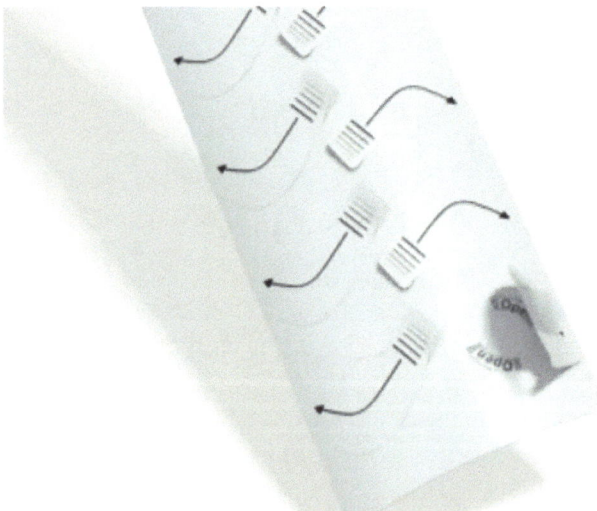

STEP III

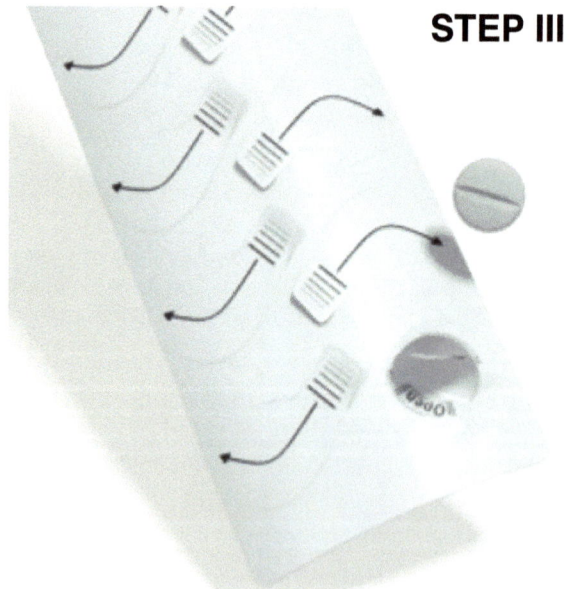

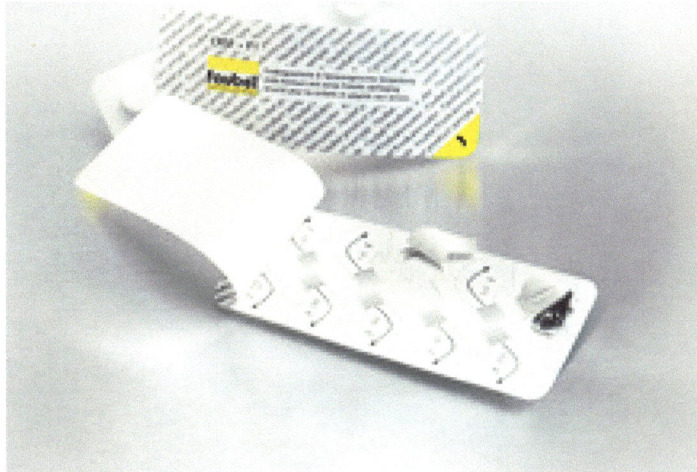

Manufacturer/Designer

Faubel & Co. Nachf. GmbHSchwarzenberger Weg 45

34212 MelsungenGermany

Phone: +49 5661 7309-0

Fax: +49 5661 7309-149

Email: info@faubel.de

http://www.faubel.de/

• The Faubel-CRSF solution is a complex safety element which can be applied like a label on the top face of a blister package. Safety is achieved via mechanical and logical barrier levels.

• This label has three mechanical and logical barrier level of safety integrated

• First is blister length pull tab which has a indication at the edge and convenient and intuitive handling by senior citizens

• Second is a individual tablet overwrap

• Third is the blister lidding

• There is a growing demand for child-resistant and senior-friendly packaging. Medication packages have to be child-safe on the one hand and easy to open for adults, on the other hand.

• The CRSF label is certified to EU standard DIN EN 14375 and US 16 CRF § 1700.20.

A single unit · 12 ml

centimeters

0   10   20   30

10 units

Shown here with Olive Oil & Balsamic Vinegar

PHARMACEUTICAL PACKAGING INNOVATIONS

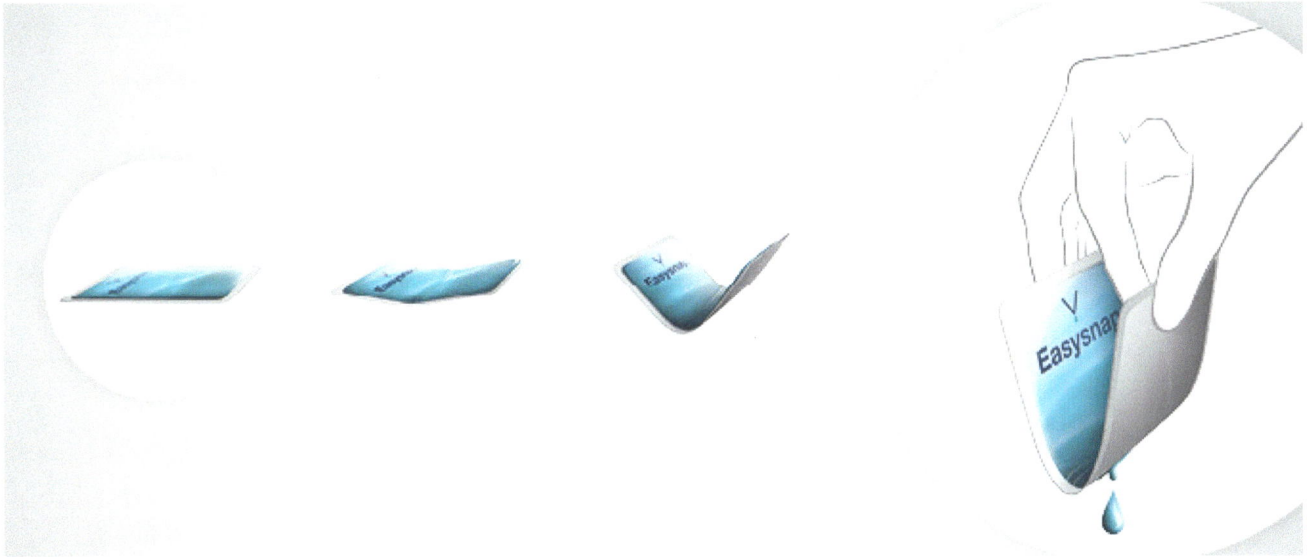

Manufacturer/Designer

Easypack Solutions S.r.l.
Via Davia 9/D, 40017
San Giovanni in Persiceto —Bologna
Italy
Ph. (+39)051.68.10.804
Fax (+39)051950091
info@easysnap.com
www.easysnap.com/en/

• Easysnap is an innovative patented and revolutional monodose packaging concept (portion pack from 1 to 25 ml) may be a replacement of any conventional sachet.

• It can contain from 2 to 30 ml liquid or semi-dense product.

• With its one hand opening system, Easysnap is suitable to open and dispense in a clean way any liquid product.

• Works with a monodose sachet, with no air inside and consequently with a long shelf-life, with an undoubtedly unique appeal and a versatility.

• Easysnap monodose sachet can be kept single in your pocket or carry bags; without the risk of leakage

•Easysnap has an ergonomic design, versatile and stylish, which you can customize in shape and graphics.

PHARMACEUTICAL PACKAGING INNOVATIONS

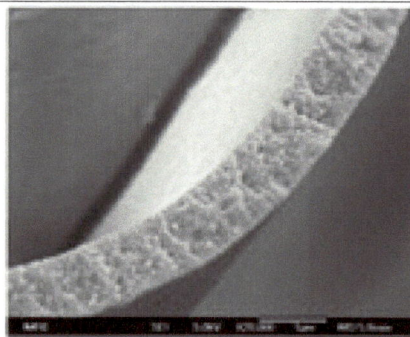

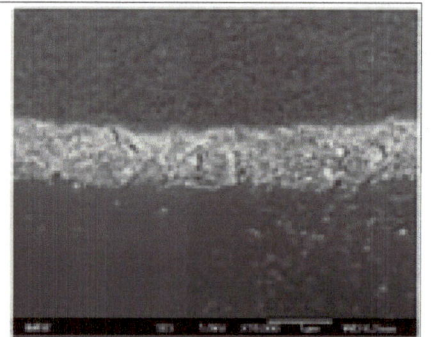

PHARMACEUTICAL PACKAGING INNOVATIONS

Manufacturer/Designer

Agency For Science, Technology And Research (A*STAR)
1 Fusionopolis Way, #20-10 Connexis North Tower, Singapore 138632
Tel: (65) 6826 6111
Fax: (65) 6777 1711
Website: www.a-star.edu.
mail: contact@a-star.edu.sg

• Tera-Barrier Films (TBF) is using a nanotechnology to produce an encapsulation barrier plastic film which could fill a hole in the market between aluminium foil and transparent oxide films, an alternative to aluminium foil.

• By installing a nanoparticle barrier in its films TBF have been able to deliver a barrier that is 10 times more effective than existing transparent oxide films at preventing air and moisture entering a pack as well as being very thin (700 nm).

• Researchers at the University of Tokyo have confirmed that the new product has a moisture vapour transmission rate of 5g/m2 day.

• It would be cheaper, and is both stretchable and transparent for the niche applications in the food, medical, pharmaceuticals and electronics markets.

E-Pharma Trento's Blister Pack

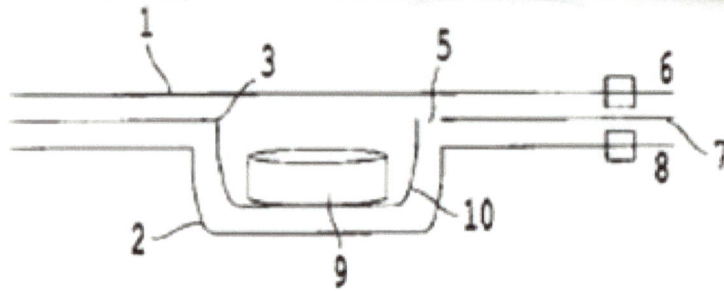

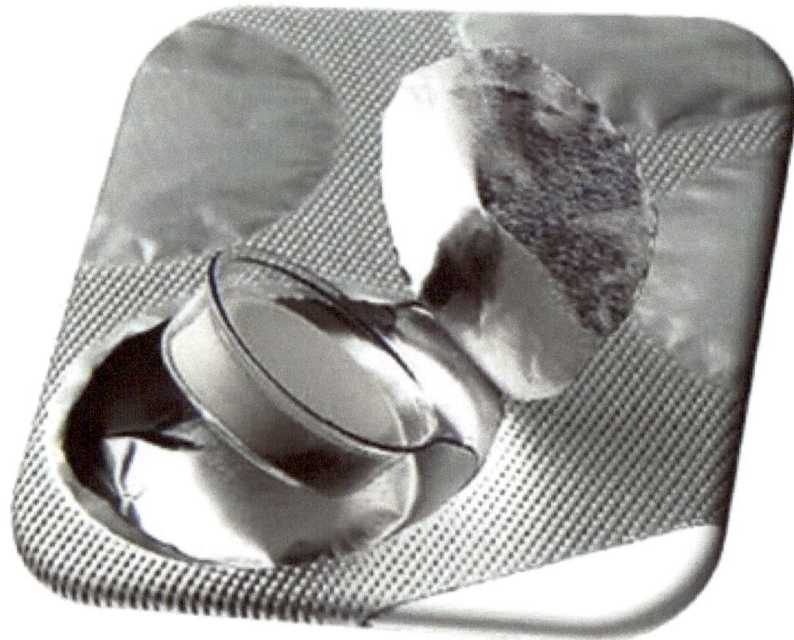

[1] European Patent Application EP 2 353 573 A1
[2] US Patent Application No. 2011/0192,759
Canadian Patent Application No. CA 2730464

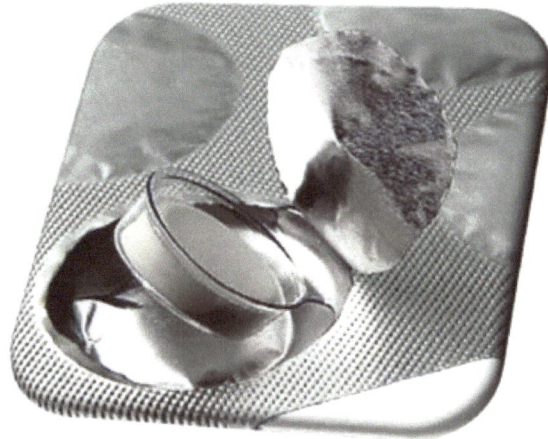

Manufacturer/Designer

E-PHARMA TRENTO S.p.A
via Provina 2
38123 Trento (Italy)
Tel: +39 (0)461 922818
Fax:+39 (0)461 922820
Email: info@epharma.it
www.e-pharmatrento.com/en/

• E-Pharma Trento's blister pack to package solid pharmaceutical and nutraceutical forms, providing special use for fragile tablets.

•The blister comprises one extra cavity of PVC in between lidding and forming.

• Made of three layers (Al - PVC - PA/Al/PVC) that make the capsule packaging more rigid, it allows the user to push-through tablets without damaging them.

• An alternative that addresses the disadvantages of existing fragile tablet packaging.

• It is patented by EU ,patent pending in US and Canada.

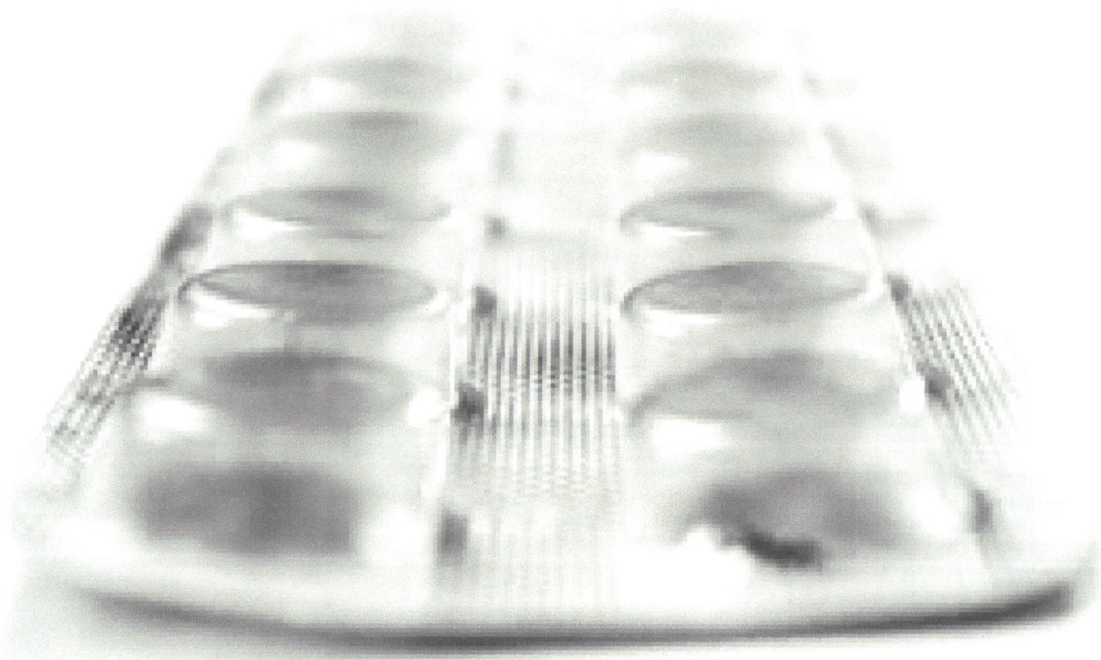

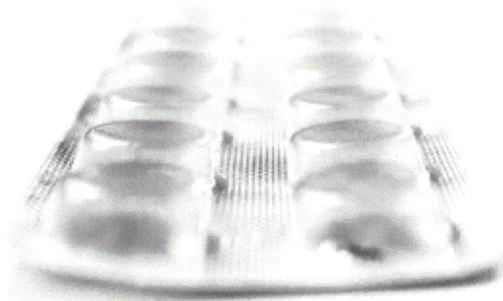

Manufacturer/Designer

Huhtamaki Films US

Huhtamaki Films, Inc.

2400 Continental Blvd.

Malvern, PA 19355

USA

Tel.: +1 484 527 2000

Fax.: +1 484 527 2100

Mail: info.malvern@us.huhtamaki.com

• COC films for blister films in the pharmaceutical sector

• Excellent mechanical properties

• Excellent transparency

• Very good barrier properties e.g against water vapor

• Very good thermomechanical properties

• Printable

• These materials comprise of COC film in gauges 120, 190, 240 and 300 mic. as barrier layer co-extruded with PP layers on both the sides. The lidding foil for sealing to PP

• COC materials can be considered as an anti-counterfeiting packaging solution since these are not available from other sources but only from authorized convertors of COC films

Activ-blister® Technology

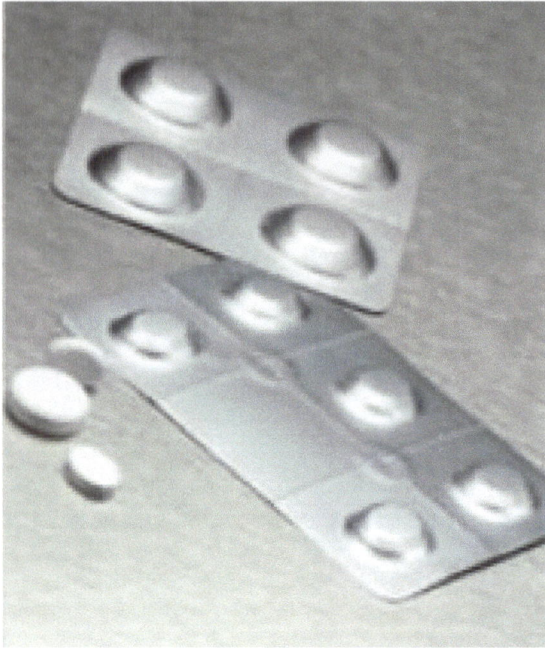

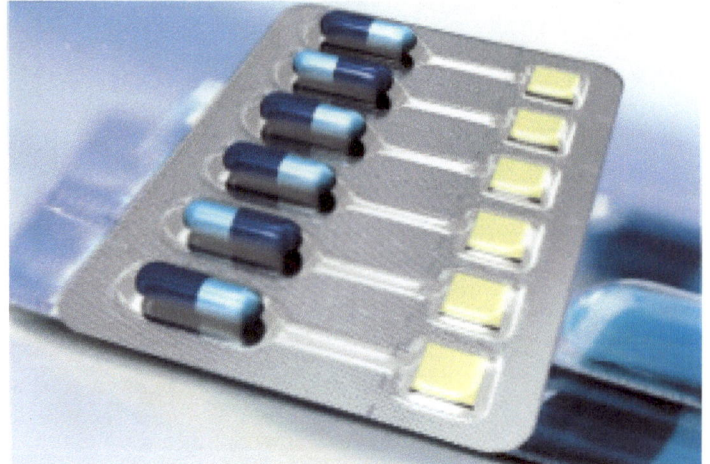

Manufacturer/Designer

CSP Technologies, Inc.
960 W. Veterans Blvd., Auburn,
AL 36832
Phone: +1 (334) 887-8300
info@csptechnologies.com.
www.csptechnologies.com/

• CSP's Activ-Blister® technology controls the internal atmosphere of each blister cavity, allowing for better product performance and shelf-life.

• Activ-Blister® can be produced in virtually every shape, offering superior flexibility in packaging design.

• Activ-Blister® solves product protection concerns related to buffering humidity and removing moisture, oxygen and odors.

• Product protection compatible with:

Push Through / Peel Blisters

Sachets/ Pouches

Stick Packs

High Barrier Foils, including both coldform and thermoform

Moisture absorption capacity: up to 20mg

Oxygen Scavenging: up to 30cc

Manufacturer/Designer

Essentra Packaging
Via Copernico, 54,
29027 I Casoni di Gariga,
Podenzano PC,
Italy
Tel: +39 0523 523901
Fax: +39 0523 523999
info@essentrapackaging.com

• The state-of-the-art Class 100,000 standard cleanroom for printing blister pack foils offers capability and the flexibility to print onto a range of different foils.

• Meet individual customer specifications, including child resistance and multi-colour flexographical print.

• Blister pack foils can be printed in up to six colour on a range of different foils and thickness

PHARMACEUTICAL PACKAGING INNOVATIONS

Manufacturer/Designer

Constantia Flexibles International GmbH

Rivergate, Handelkai 92

1200 Wien, Austria

T +43 1 888 56 40 1000

F +43 1 888 56 40 1900

Email: office(at)cflex.com

www.cflex.com

• Constantia Flexibles 's easy-PIESY Blister Lidding a paper-free, child-resistant blister lidding foil with upgraded peel/push functionalities for consumers and an efficient packaging process for manufacturers.

• Offering a smooth, robust peel, the an Al. Foil/PET/Al.Foil lamination that — due to its absence of paper — requires less heat during the sealing process than traditional paper-back foil structures.

• The result is superior heat transmission through the laminate, which leads to higher productivity and less stress on machines.

• The paper-free design also makes it especially suited to cleanroom environments, and easy-PIESY can be adopted without additional tooling or modifications to existing heat-seal lacquer.

PHARMACEUTICAL PACKAGING INNOVATIONS

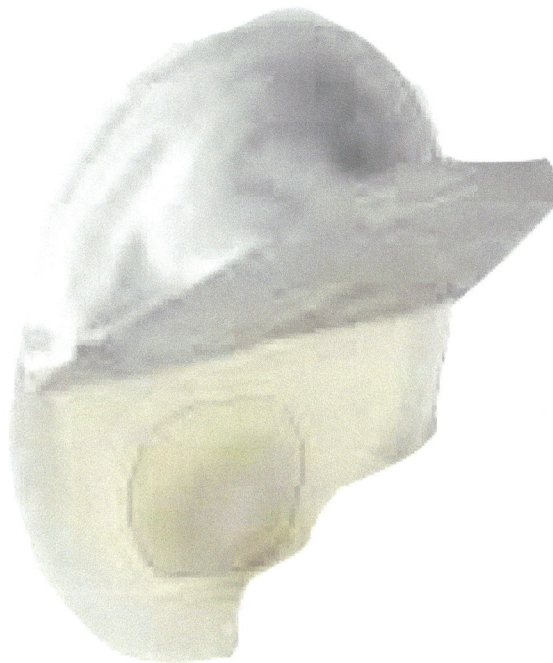

Manufacturer/Designer

Constantia Flexibles International GmbH

Rivergate, Handelkai 92

1200 Wien, Austria

T +43 1 888 56 40 1000

F +43 1 888 56 40 1900

Email: office(at)cflex.com

www.cflex.com

• Constantia Flexibles' Dispense Lid is developed as a means of dosing tablets, capsules or liquids from plastic bottles in a controlled and more compliant manner.

• Incorporated into a bottle's closure, the Dispense Lid features a liner with a small opening that induction seals to high-density polyethylene, polypropylene, and polystyrene bottles.

• The customized opening feature helps users dispense only the desired number of tablets or capsules, assisting with compliance and minimizing the risk of contamination to remaining product.

• The Dispense Lid is highly difficult to copy and, therefore, also aids in anti-counterfeiting measures.

PHARMACEUTICAL PACKAGING INNOVATIONS

Manufacturer/Designer

Rockwell Solutions Limited
Brunel Road Dundee. DD2 4TG,
United Kingdom
Tel: 44 (0) 1382 622122
Fax: 44 (0) 1382 623089
Email: sales@rockwellsolutions.com
www.rockwellsolutions.com

- The Rocklid Induction Sealing Conductive Liner to seal to any substrate to achieve a peel or a weld seal.
- The benefits of the solution include consistent hermetic sealing for greater protection and no leaks
- Peelable seals at 0.1 seconds; a clean, smooth peel, with no film tear; and no 'stringing' or residue.
- It also offers good product preservation because of its high moisture and gas barrier, a high degree of tamper evidence and prevention of tainting, while delivering cost savings compared to alternative laminates.
- Rocklid-CL liners can be removed cleanly and easily in one piece and are available with or without residue once removed from the container.
- Rockwell also supply 100% compostable and biodegradable liners with our proprietary Biopeel coating on PLA film.

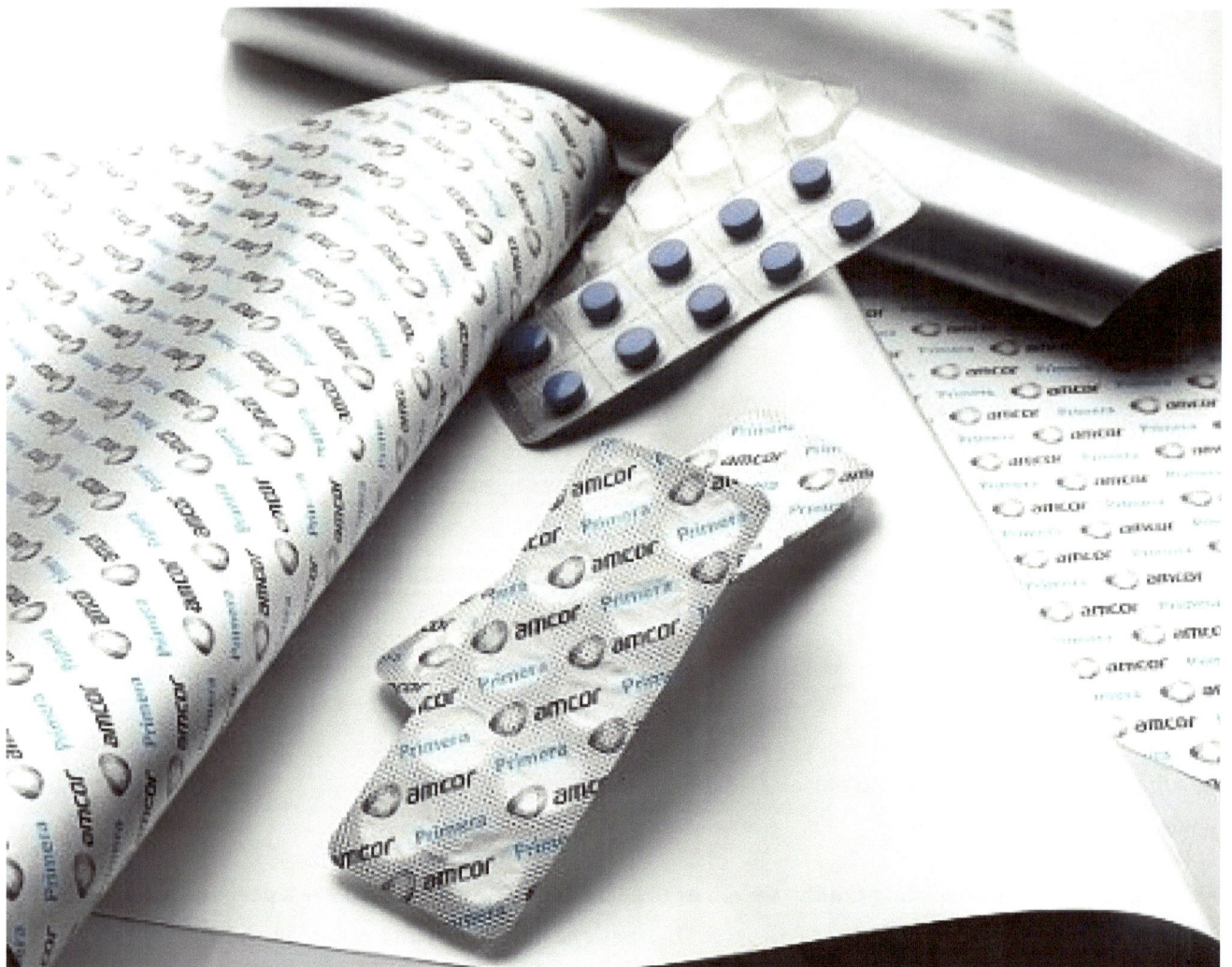

PHARMACEUTICAL PACKAGING INNOVATIONS

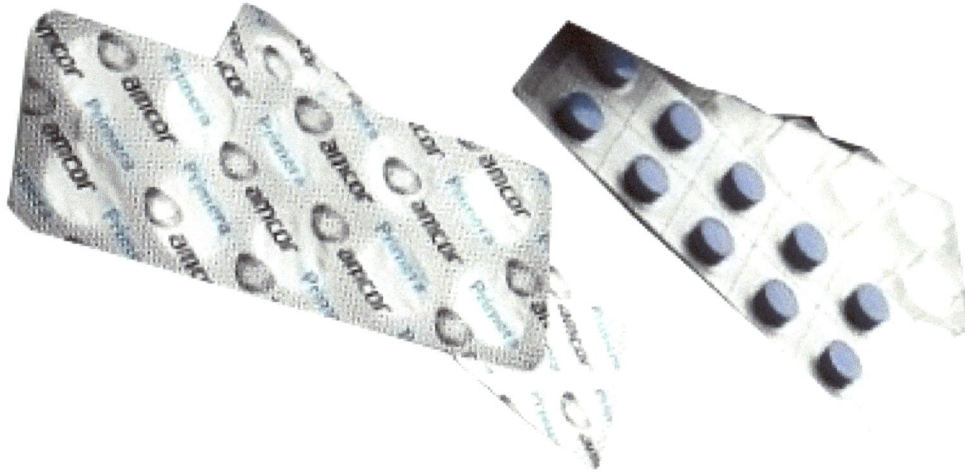

Manufacturer/Designer

AMCOR FLEXIBLES
HAWKFIELD Way,bristol,avon,
BS14 0BD, United Kingdom
Tel: +44 1179753200
Fax: +44 1179753311
Email: sales@amcor.com

• Primera Lid Foil, a unique push-through foil with a print primer that performs on all current printing technologies and inks.

• Primera is first in its class for thermal resistance, and it features a smooth, high quality printing surface. To date, no single specification has been able to meet the high demands of different printing technologies, which has increased complexity in the blister market.

• Primera was given full release by the Swiss printing solutions company HAPA for ink systems 26, 38, 39, 78 dorp on demand (DOD), 78 Webjet and 80 ULP. This makes it the first and only primer to achieve a release across this many systems, while continuing to deliver premium results on standard rotogravure, flexo, UV-flexo as well as CSAT, Wolke and Atlantic Zeiser systems.

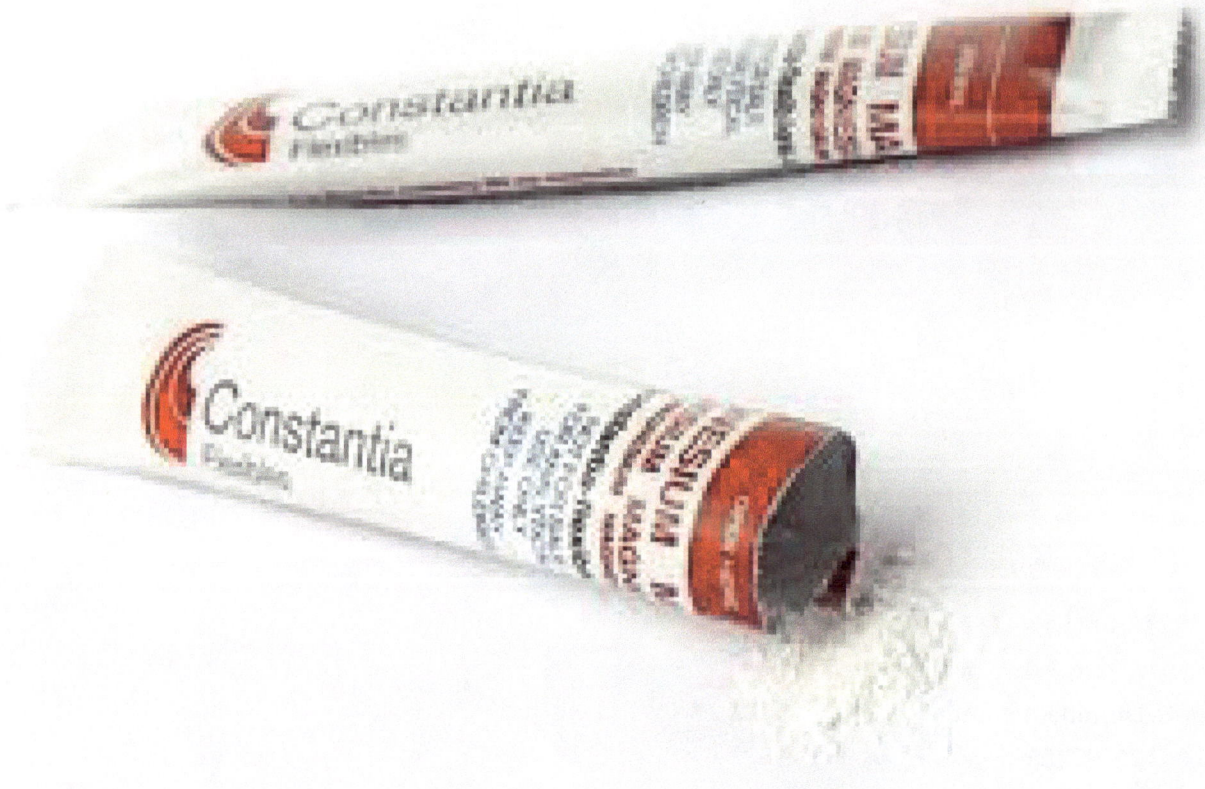

Manufacturer/Designer

Constantia Flexibles International GmbH
Rivergate, Handelkai 92
1200 Wien, Austria
T +43 1 888 56 40 1000
F +43 1 888 56 40 1900
Email: office(at)cflex.com
www.cflex.com

• Constantia Flexibles's laser-perforated stick pack materials whose foil laminate comprises PET/AL/PE or even paper/AL/PE to protect the contents against moisture, oxygen and light.

• A laser perforation below the seal ensures easy opening of the stick.

• The PET or paper in the area of the laser seam is partially removed and the aluminum layer remains intact, thereby ensuring the impermeability of the stick.

• Other features include a pre-determined breaking point for convenient and easy-to-open packaging; an integrated perforation of packaging — so no equipment modifications are necessary; a flexible perforation-layout to accommodate varying customer needs; and child-resistant options and capabilities.

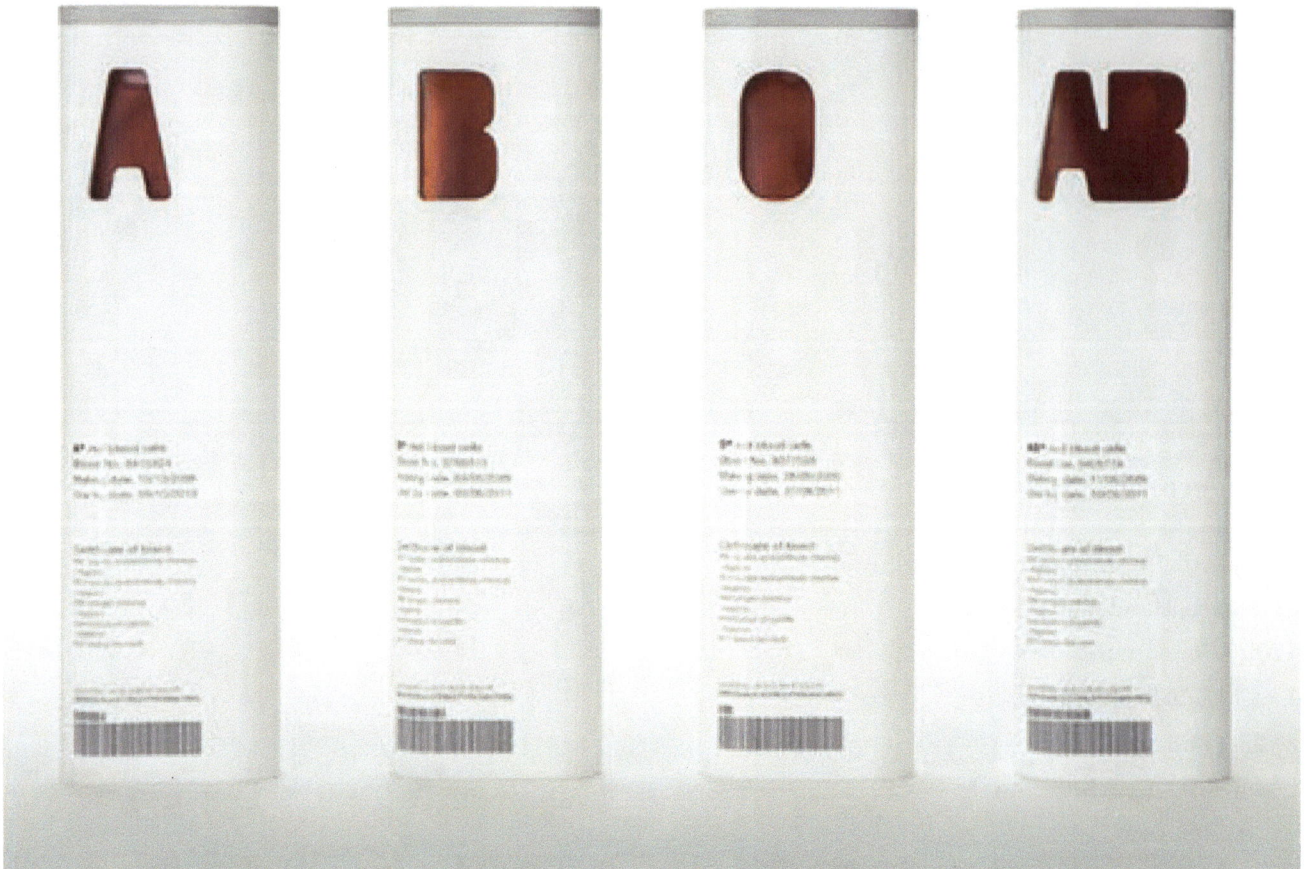

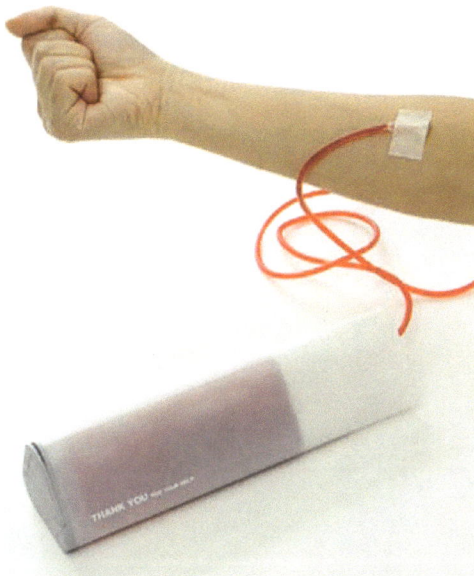

Manufacturer/Designer

Designer: Jihye Lee

• The Sweet Donation Bag is an attempt to redesign the blood collection pouch.

• It features a sleeve with large cut-outs indicating the blood type (A, B, AB & O).

• The overall design is much more refined than the current bags in use and the packaging looks sturdy.

• Designer Jihye Lee proposes a different look for blood collection bags featuring a more solid construction, large labeling of blood type

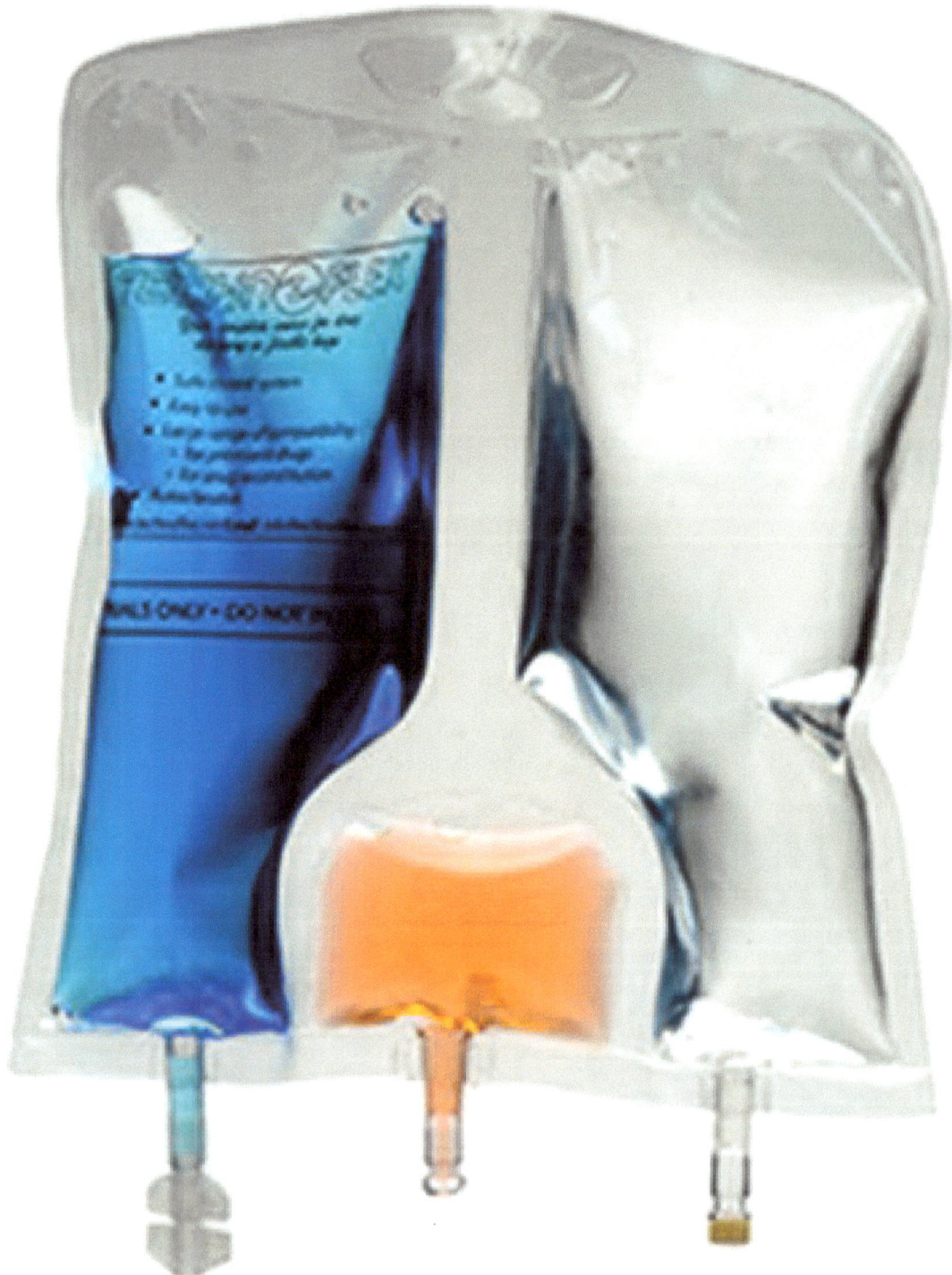

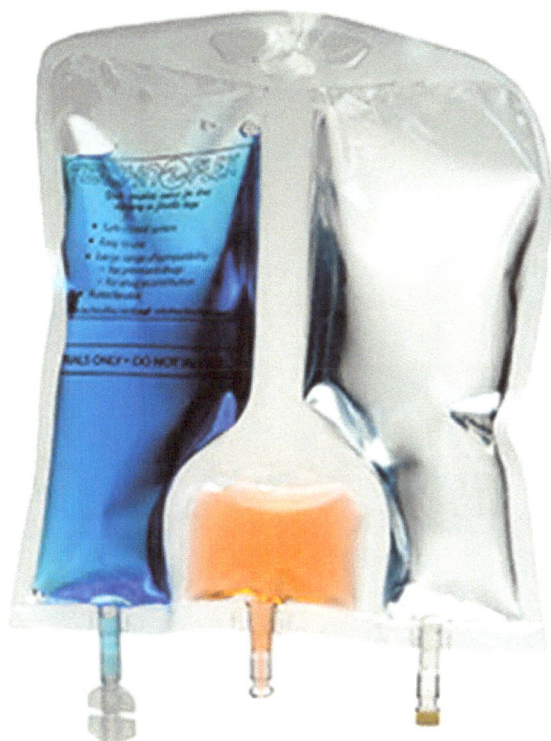

Manufacturer/Designer

Technoflex ZA de
Bassilour
64210 BIDART
France
Tél. : +33(0)5 59 54 66 66
Fax : +33(0)5 59 54 90 06
info@technoflex.net
sales@technoflex.net
invest@technoflex.net
rh@technoflex.net

• Technoflex offers whole a range of multi-chamber bags - double, triple or customized - for different applications such as parenteral nutrition or drug reconstitution.

• It is suitable for drugs which are certainly more highly complex & that require tailor-made packaging.

• These DEHP-free or polypropylene IV bags have been designed to allow the separation of different solutions that require mixing just before administration to the patient.

• The chambers are separated by a divisible connector or peelable welds.

• In this last case, the solutions are mixed by simply squeezing one of the chambers manually.

PHARMACEUTICAL PACKAGING INNOVATIONS

PHARMACEUTICAL PACKAGING INNOVATIONS

Manufacturer/Designer

Hoffmann Neopac AG

Burgdorfstrasse 22

Postfach

3672 Oberdiessbach

Switzerland

T: +41 (0)31 770 11 11

F: +41 (0)31 770 13 13

Email: info(at)neopac.com

http://www.neopac.com/

• Fleximed transparent, flexible medical tubes offer an alternative to glass for parenteral packaging.

• Offer ease of use, reliability, and safety of medical administration.

• Eliminates the need for syringes to release medication from the vial. Fleximed Easymix is a tube with two or more chambers to mix different dry and liquid components.

• Made of silicon and tungsten-free materials, tubes may be sterilized using radiation.

• Easymix offers the unique ability to mix two or more components just before administration.

• Full flexibility to choose size of each chamber based on fill volumes.

• Liquid/liquid or liquid/powder combinations possible.

• The chambers are devided by a tight peeling strip.

• Easy to mix by pressure onto the chambers.

PHARMACEUTICAL PACKAGING INNOVATIONS

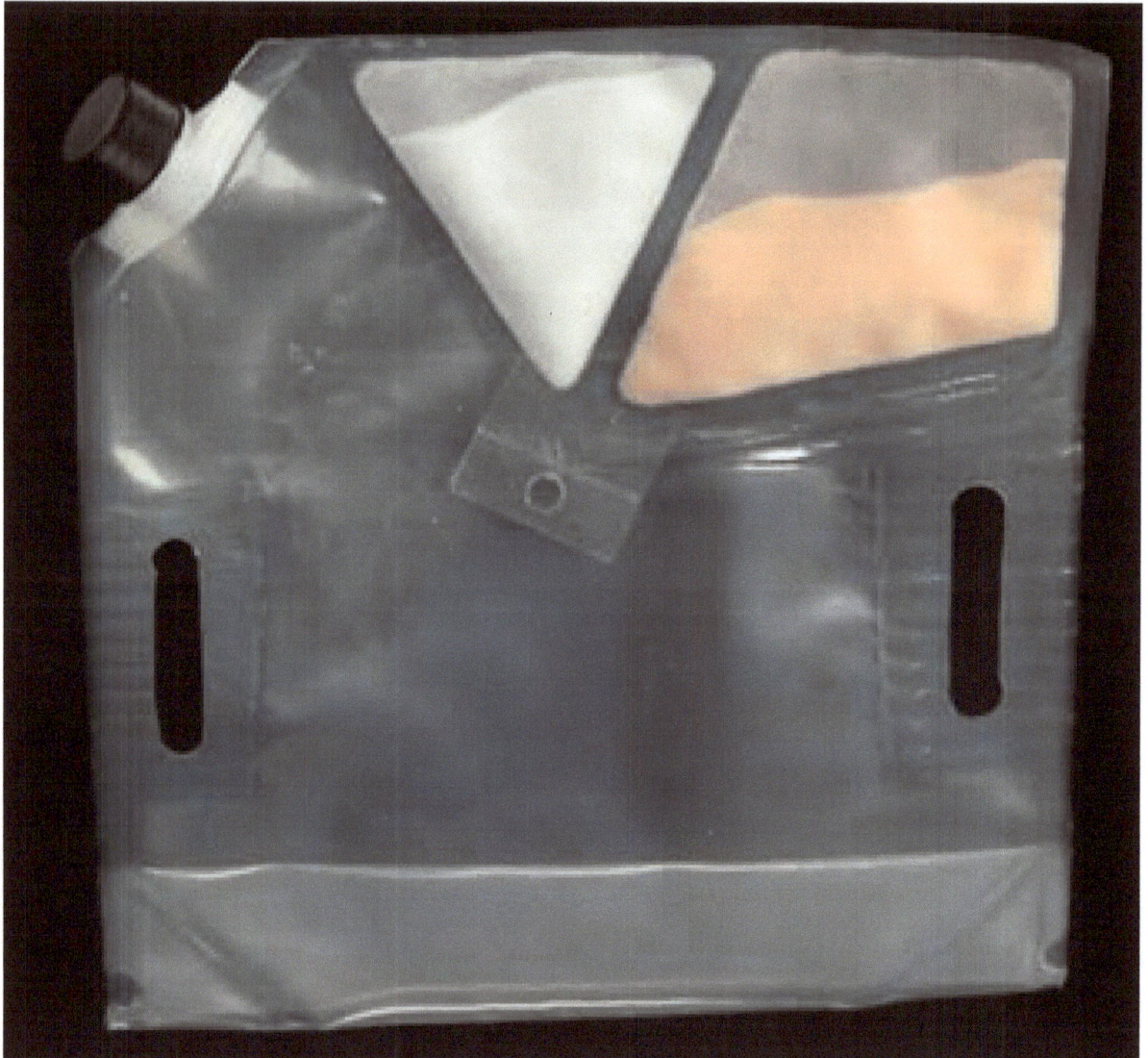

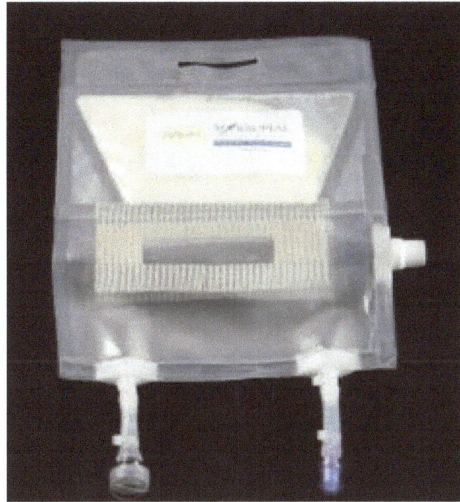

Manufacturer/Designer

LiDestri Food & Beverage
Alan Davis
Vice President, Business Development & Contract Manufacturing
Phone: 585.388.4122,
davidd@lidestrifoods.com

• Multi-compartment flexible plastic container that may have several segregated compartments, where the seal or seals may be ruptured and the contents mixed.

• The packaging can hold product mixes including powder and powder, liquid and powder, liquid and liquid, powder/liquid, and empty.

• Contents are kept separate prior to mixing, maintaining quality, freshness, and tast

• Preportioned medication mixture for nursing or pharmacy staff

• Easy to use and operate, even for those with dexterity challenge

• Multi-port/spout options

• Stand-up, lay-flat, or hang/IV design

• Large graphic/text area

• Individual or unit-dose customization

• Antibiotic delivery/administration

• Shelf space advantages in space-limited markets such as urban and/or Europe

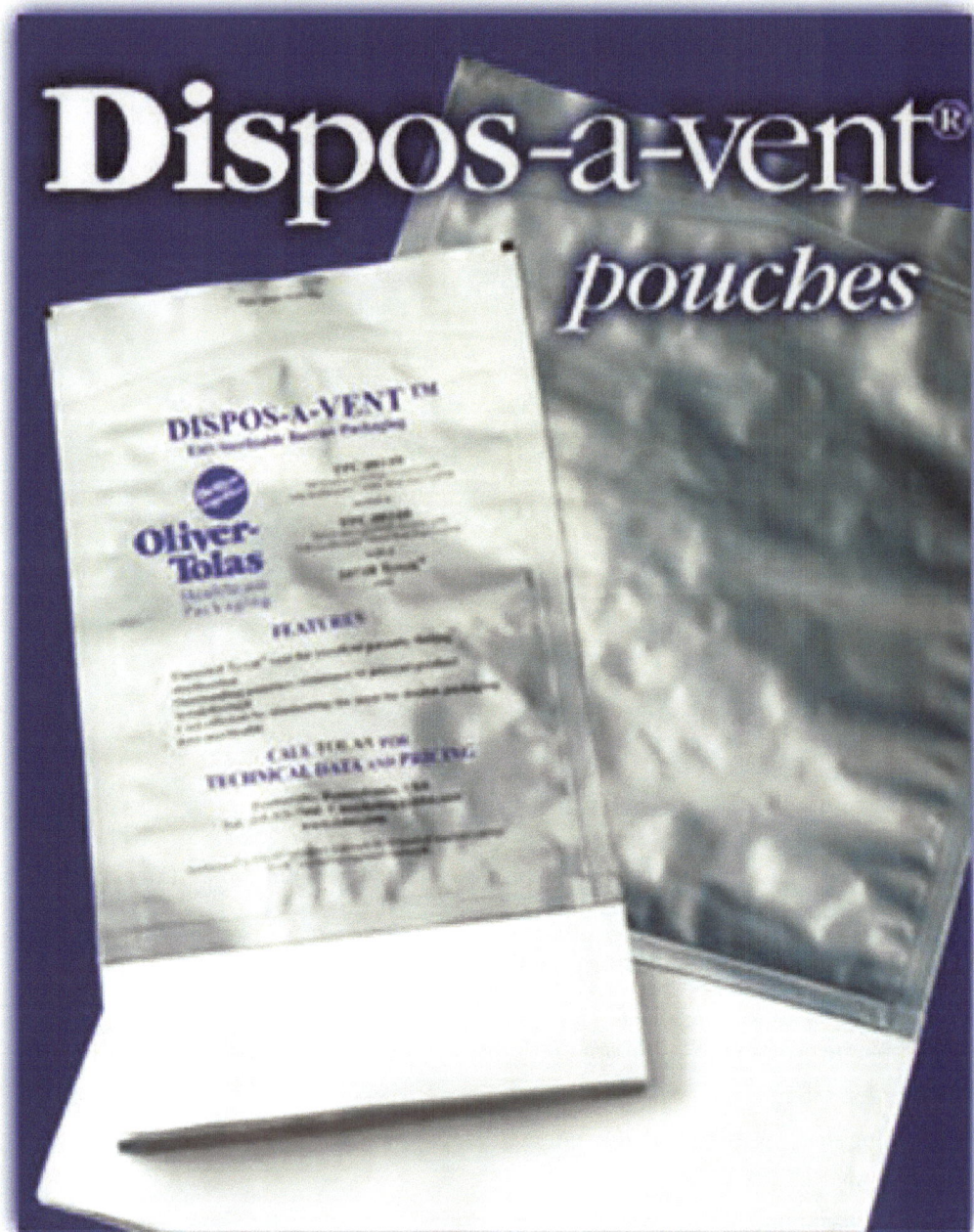

PHARMACEUTICAL PACKAGING INNOVATIONS

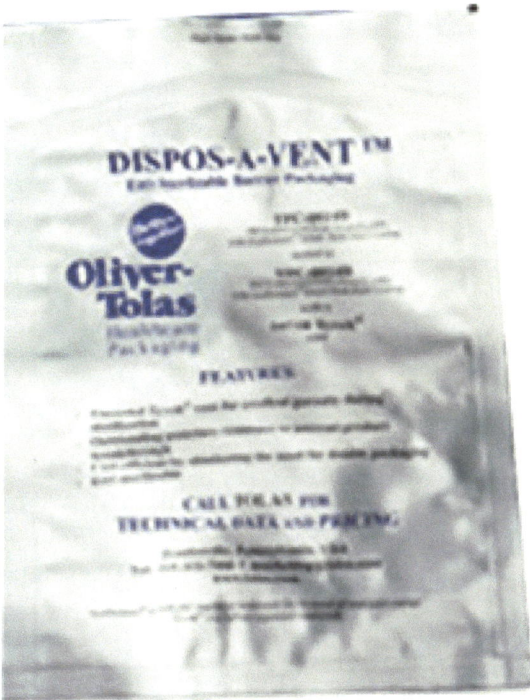

Manufacturer/Designer

Oliver-Tolas® locations
445 Sixth Street,
NWGrand Rapids,
MI 49504 USA
877.283.3431 toll-free
Tel.: 616.456.7711 Fax: 616.456.5820
Email: info@olover-tolas.com

Dispos-a-vent® barrier pouches are designed with a disposable Tyvek® or paper vent for maximum airflow during EtO or steam sterilization and a spacious high barrier film or foil pouch area for easy conversion after sterilization.

• Sterile device in a film or foil pouch with superior barrier properties.
• **Features:**
• Oxygen barrier for protection of sensitive product.

• Moisture barrier for prolonged shelf life
• Other barrier properties depend on material combination selected
• Uncoated Tyvek® or paper vent for excellent porosity during sterilization
• Outstanding puncture resistance to prevent product breakthrough
• Cost efficient by eliminating the need for double packaging
• Peelable seal pouches feature Oliver-Tolas' SealScience® heat-seal coating technology, for visual assurance of seal integrity (also available as tear-open pouches)

CLOSURE & DISPENSING SOLUTIONS

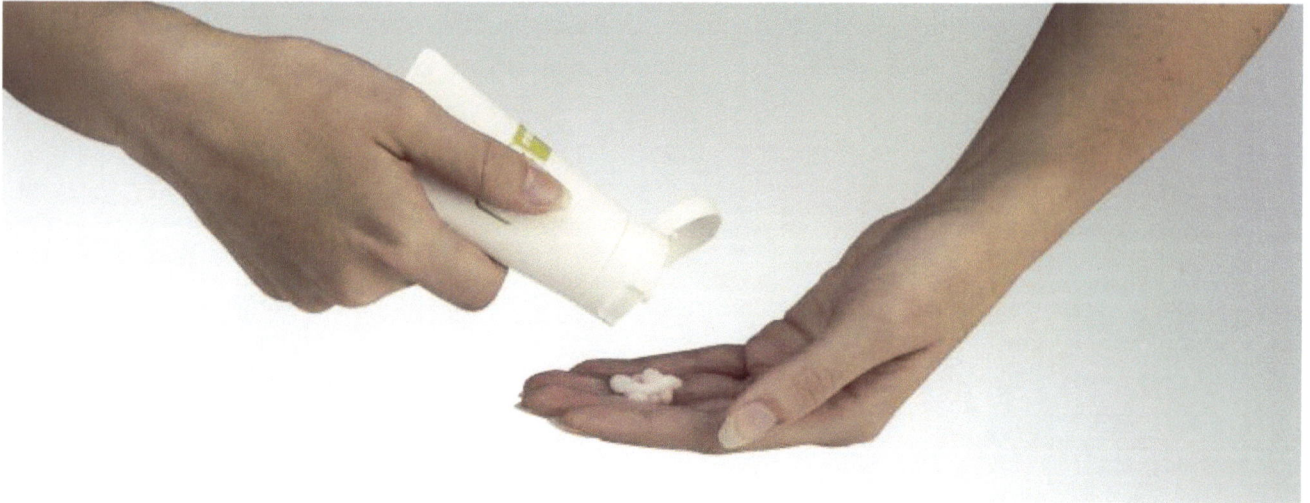

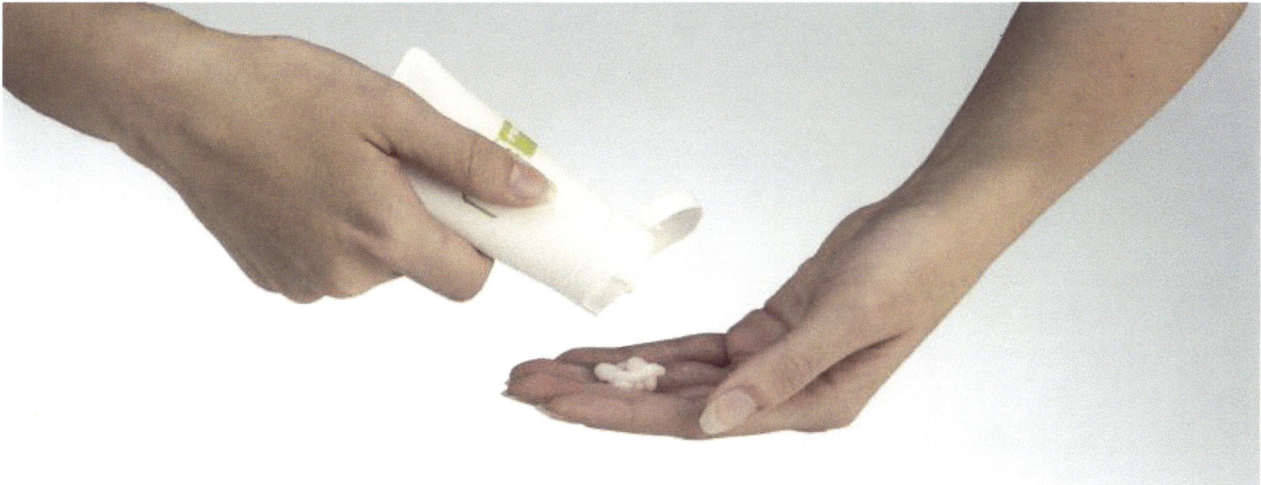

Manufacturer/Designer

Clariant
Rothausstrasse 61
4132 Muttenz, Switzerland
Tel: 41 61 469 63 63
Email: info@clariant.com
www.clariant.com

• Tubairless®, an innovative airless packaging system for protecting and dispensing sensitive pharmaceutical semi-solids and creams.

• Packaging keeps its original shape, integrity and legibility, while product waste is minimized with greater than 95% evacuation.

• Clariant's Healthcare Packaging has partnered with PumpArt System® to introduce Tubairless®.

• Tubairless combines an air chamber and a soft plastic pouch sealed in a flexible tube.

• The dispensing system helps protect sensitive cream-based formulas from the adverse effects of outside air.

• The tube's internal pump prevents air intake and product flow-back during dispensing, reducing the ingress of unwanted elements that can contaminate the contents. Protection can be further enhanced by integrating multiple protective barrier or active layers into the package.

• The Tubairless design can help address preservation issues as formulators look for ways to reduce or eliminate preservatives from formulations.

PHARMACEUTICAL PACKAGING INNOVATIONS

Manufacturer/Designer

Sanner Deutschland Sanner GmbH
Schillerstraße 76
64625 Bensheim, Germany
Tel.   +49(0)6251 938-0
Fax +49(0)6251 74672
info@sanner-group.com
www.sanner-group.com

• Brilliance®Tube for effervescent tablets with in-mold labeling (IML) and the desiccant closures offers customers a complete solution.

• Photorealistic printing for more attention at the retail and more legible product information. Various surface structure up to 8 colors, metallic effects.

• Impact- and scratch-resistant decoration

• Best suited for effervescent tablets, but also works with conventional or coated tablets and other solid pharmaceutical products.

• Manufactured using IML technology, the packaging offers customers a wide range of design options and a premium-quality appearance.

• Protect contents perfectly against light and moisture.

• The geometry of the tube base ensures that the tubes can be easily packaged in standard commercial sales trays.

Pure Dispense Technology

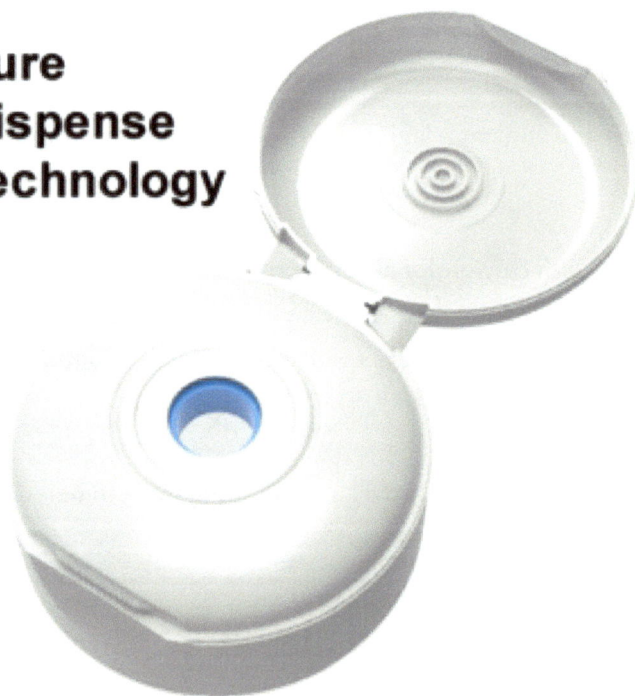

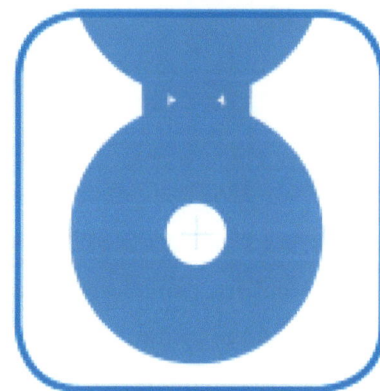

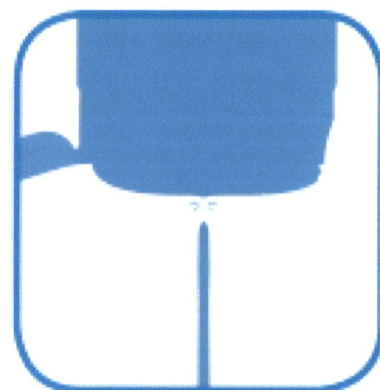

Membrane solution for a pure and controlled dispense

**Pure
Dispense
Technology**

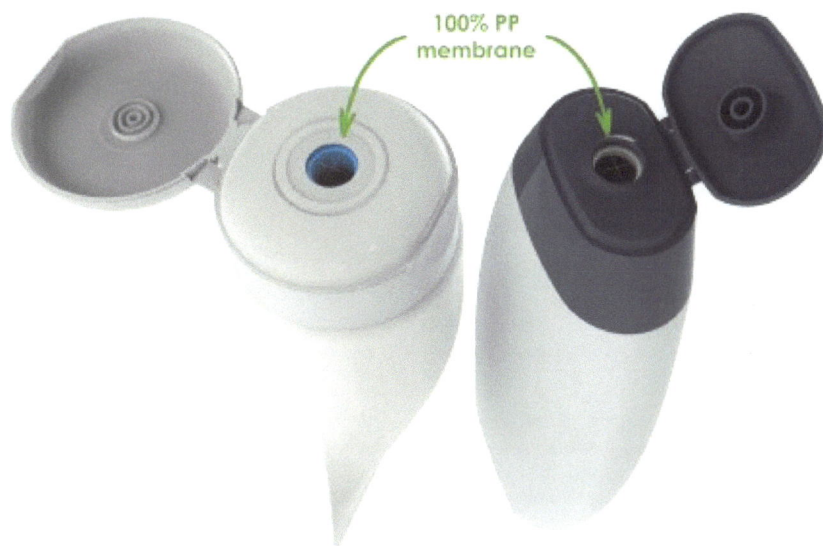

100% PP membrane

Manufacturer/Designer

Weener Plastik GmbH
Industriestr. 1
26826 Weener, Germany
Phone: +49 4951 306-0
Fax: +49 4951 306-150
http://www.wppg.com
info@wppg.com

• A new patented cost-effective dosing system

• Pure Dispense is an applied membrane presenting a sustainable solution for an accurate and controlled dispense of various formulations, due to the efficient and direct movement of the membrane when squeezing the tube or bottle.

• This patented membrane technology can be integrated in standard as well as customized dispensing closures.

• The membrane is even suitable for the contemporary flexible and thin walled

• Containers, since they quickly return into their original shape after use.

• Pure not only because of an honest dispense, but also because of the 100% polypropylene material, which implies a carefree recycling. This makes the Pure Dispense technology also environmentally friendly.

Mega Airless

Cap :	**PP**
Actuator top :	**PP**
Actuator bottom :	**PP**
Upper valve :	**EVA**
Bellows :	**LD-PE**
Cylinder / container :	**PP**
Piston :	**HD-PE**
Bottom plate :	**PP**

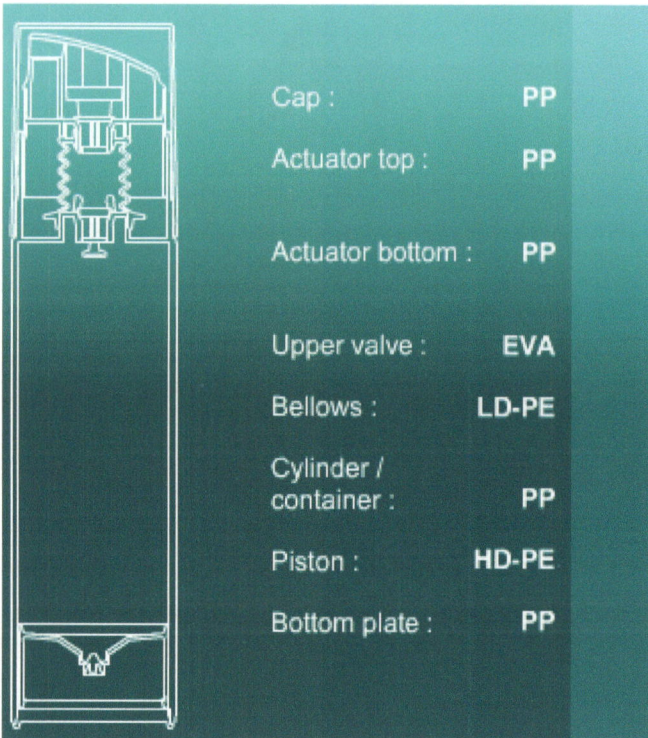

- 20 different version sizes from 30 ml to 200 ml, round or oval shaped.
- Multiple actuator and cap styles.
- Precise dosage choices of 0,5 ml, 0,8 ml, 1,0 ml and 1.5 ml.
- No metal parts - All plastic system.
- Each dispenser is 100 % function tested.
- Actuator with automatic self-sealing valve within orifice available (stops air and prevents dry-out and contamination).
- Minimal residue.
- Dispensing in any position.
- Complete range of decoration solutions (see our services).

PHARMACEUTICAL PACKAGING INNOVATIONS

Manufacturer/Designer

MEGAPLAST GMBH & CO KG

IM OBERDORF 29,

78052 VILLINGEN-SCHWENNINGEN/ OT PFAFFENWEILER,

Germany

Tel: +49 772191940

Fax: +49 77219194138

Email: info@megaplast.de

http://www.mega-airless.de/

• Airless dispensers, suitable for a variety of formulas. Has a unique patented double valve construction consistently delivers precise dosage.

• Provides complete 360-degree application, exact dosing, highly efficient evacuation and formula stability over the life of the product, without discoloration, clumping or clogging and extend product shelf life.

• All-plastic design not metal with means recyclable, that appeals to customers, retailers and today's end-users.

• Every dispenser is vacuum-tested inline and delivers precision dosing, quick-priming and 360-degree operation.

• Customize dispensing solutions and delivers superior return on investment.

PHARMACEUTICAL PACKAGING INNOVATIONS

Slider

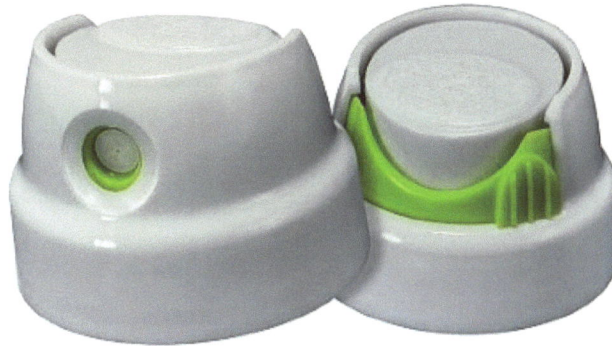

Manufacturer/Designer

APTAR GROUP SA

147 RUE DU PRÉSIDENT ROOSEVELT, B.P. 5232, 78

175 SAINT GERMAIN-EN-LAYE CÉDEX, France

Tel: +33 130871980

Fax: +33 130870909

Email: info@aptargroup.com

www.aptar.com

• Glide is Aptar's new hoodless accessory technology using the popular glide motion, the sliding motion of digital technology like iPods and smartphones.

• Glide is designed for one-hand-dispensing: Due to the ergonomics of the hand, Glide can be unlocked with a sideward movement of the thumb and actuated with the index finger.

• The grooved surface of the generous finger pad enhances ease of use.

• It´s obvious at first glance whether Glide is locked or unlocked.

• Audible clicks and a covered orifice indicate when the actuator is locked and ready to use. This unique feature provides additional assurance to consumers.

• Glide is secure when the package is locked for safe storage and portability. The lockable system with non-removable pieces provides value-added confidence for distribution and transportation before, during and after purchase.

• Compatible with many of the standard components of pumps on the market today and is available for different dispensing systems or spraying

PHARMACEUTICAL PACKAGING INNOVATIONS

Hermetic

The device is re-closable and has a «tamper evident» system for the first use.

Effective

The internal pin ensures that products to be dosed are mixed and that the system remains leaktight.

Secure

Thanks to the Twist and Close system, the medication is protected and cannot flow back into the container.

Leaktight

Leaktightness is ensured by a seal between the ring on the cannula and the container.

Made-to-measure

The cannula fits all container necks. Tailor the pin and ring to your image with the colour of your choice.

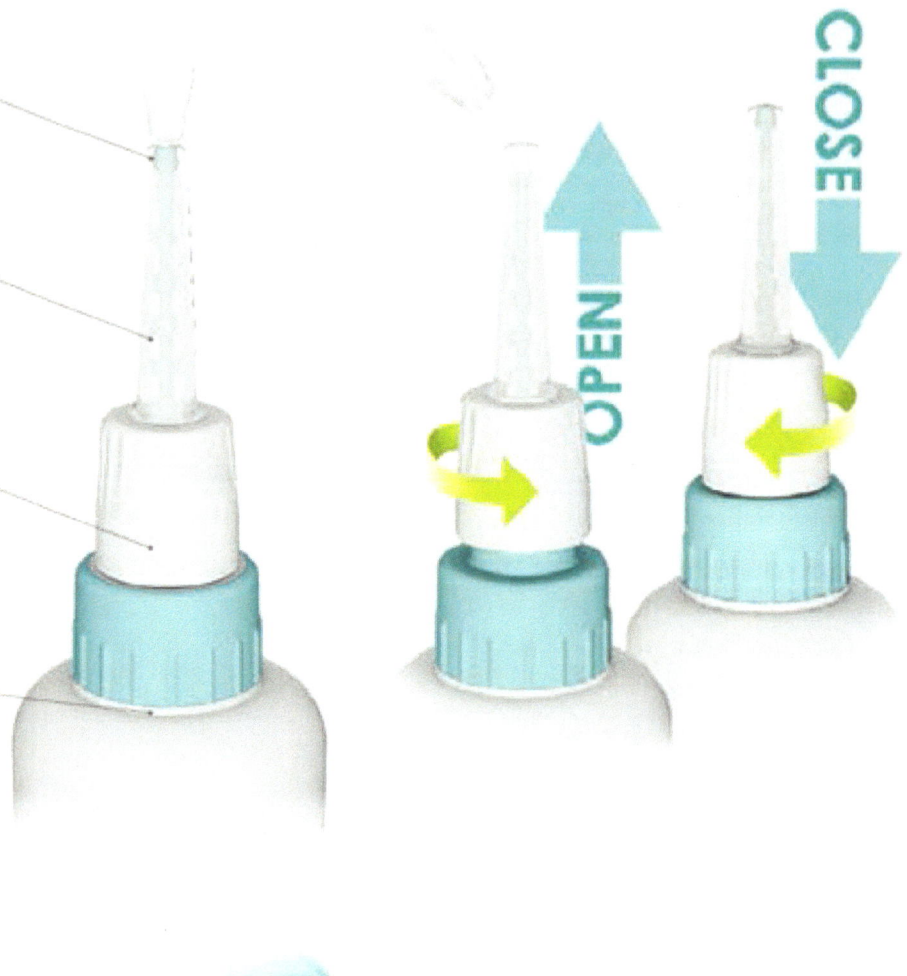

OPEN

CLOSE

PHARMACEUTICAL PACKAGING INNOVATIONS

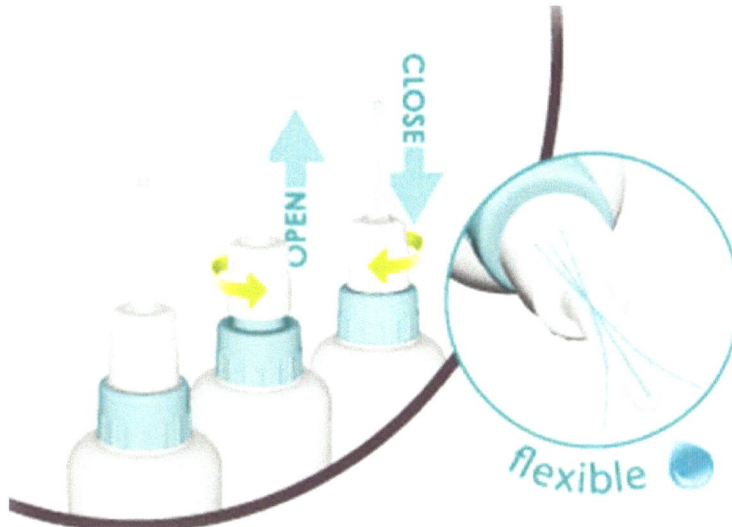

Manufacturer/Designer

Stiplastics
RD1532 - ZI Les Ors
38160 Beauvoir En Royans, France
Phone: +33 4 76380844
Fax: +33 4 76385439
http://www.stiplastics.com
sales@stiplastics.com

• Stiplastics developed a dosing devices to hit the veterinary market with a specific cannula, for veterinarian uses, pets & farm.

• It presents lots of advantages: The supple and flexible nozzle is perfect to deliver the exact dose of medicine directly inside the auditory canal without hurting the animal.

• Standard Material: Transparent PVC applicator, PET Primary Ring, PP Ring and Pin

• Tamper Evident cap: must be broken before the first use.

• Re-closable cap, system Turn & close : hermetical closure totally airtight. To dispense the medication, just do a quarter turn to open the top of tube.

• To close, re-screw the other way around and the medicine is kept safe inside the bottle. No more cap lost.

• The cannula can be easily used with a single hand. No more risk of contamination by touching th dirty nozzle with the hand to close the cap.

PHARMACEUTICAL PACKAGING INNOVATIONS

Disposable Ampoule Breaker

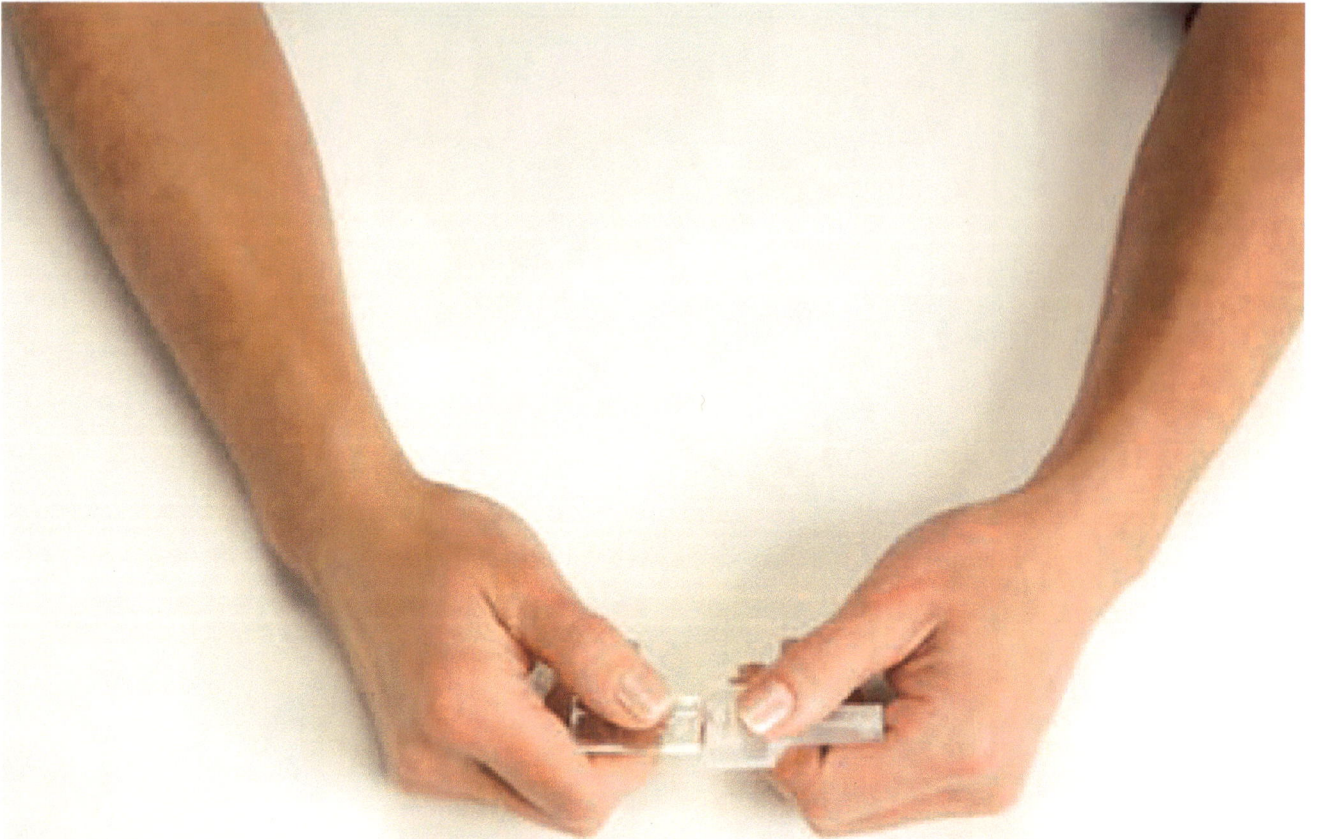

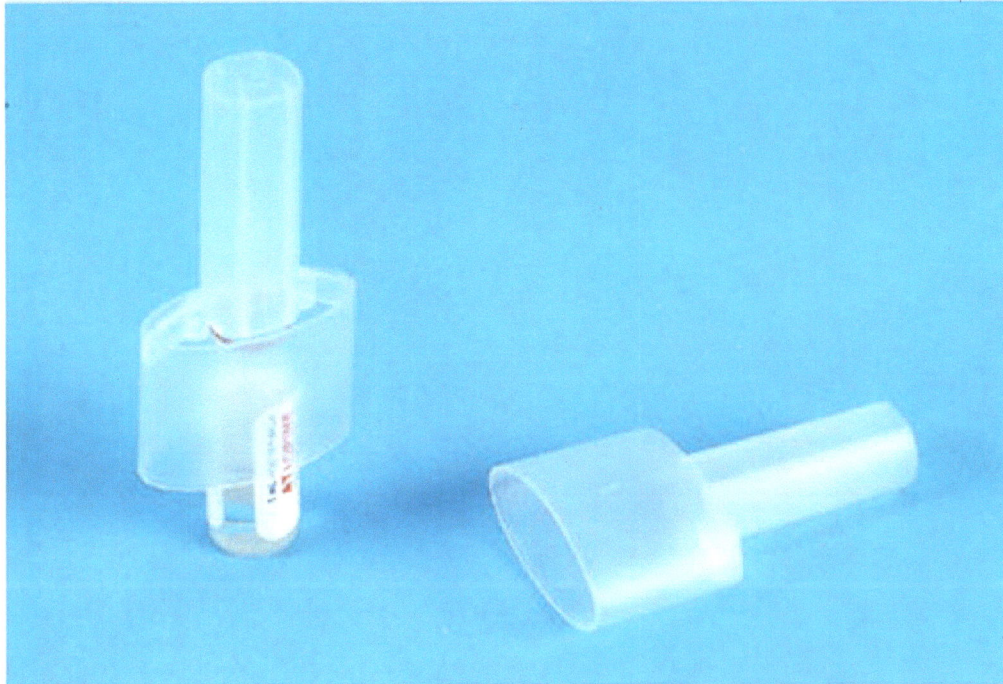

Manufacturer/Designer

EM Innovations, Inc
P.O. Box 262Galloway, OH 43119
Phone: 614/853-1504
Fax: 614/853-1104
http://www.eminnovations.com

• Safely open ampoules without finger cuts and cross-contamination.

• This unique disposable plastic breaker fits over the top of an ampoule and with a simple snap to the side, the top of the ampoule is safely removed from the base.

• The top of the ampoule can then be safely discarded with the ampoule breaker.

• The clean break reduces chances of glass splinters falling into the ampoule.

• Convenient size for med kits, pockets, and small compartments i.e. 2"L x 1-1/4"W

PHARMACEUTICAL PACKAGING INNOVATIONS

Manufacturer/Designer

Abbott Healthcare Pvt. Ltd.,
D Mart Bldg, Goregaon Mulund Link Road,
Mulund (W), Mumbai- 400080
http://www.abbottep.in/

• LiDoCon is the Liquid Dosing Concept from Abbott Healthcare (PVT), Limited.

 • LiDiCon" – a variable integrated dosing device for liquid syrups which involves 3 simple steps for accurate dosing and dispensing of liquids.

• Addressing many problems associated earlier with dosing such as possible spillage, contamination due to multiple openings/closings of bottles, maintaining separate dosing device till the last dose and cumbersome liquid dispensing steps in busy lifestyles.

• This is a simple dosing device made up of pharmaceutical grade plastic and elastomeric materials free from metal components unlike the complex spring/valve loaded mechanism.

LABELS & OUTSERTS

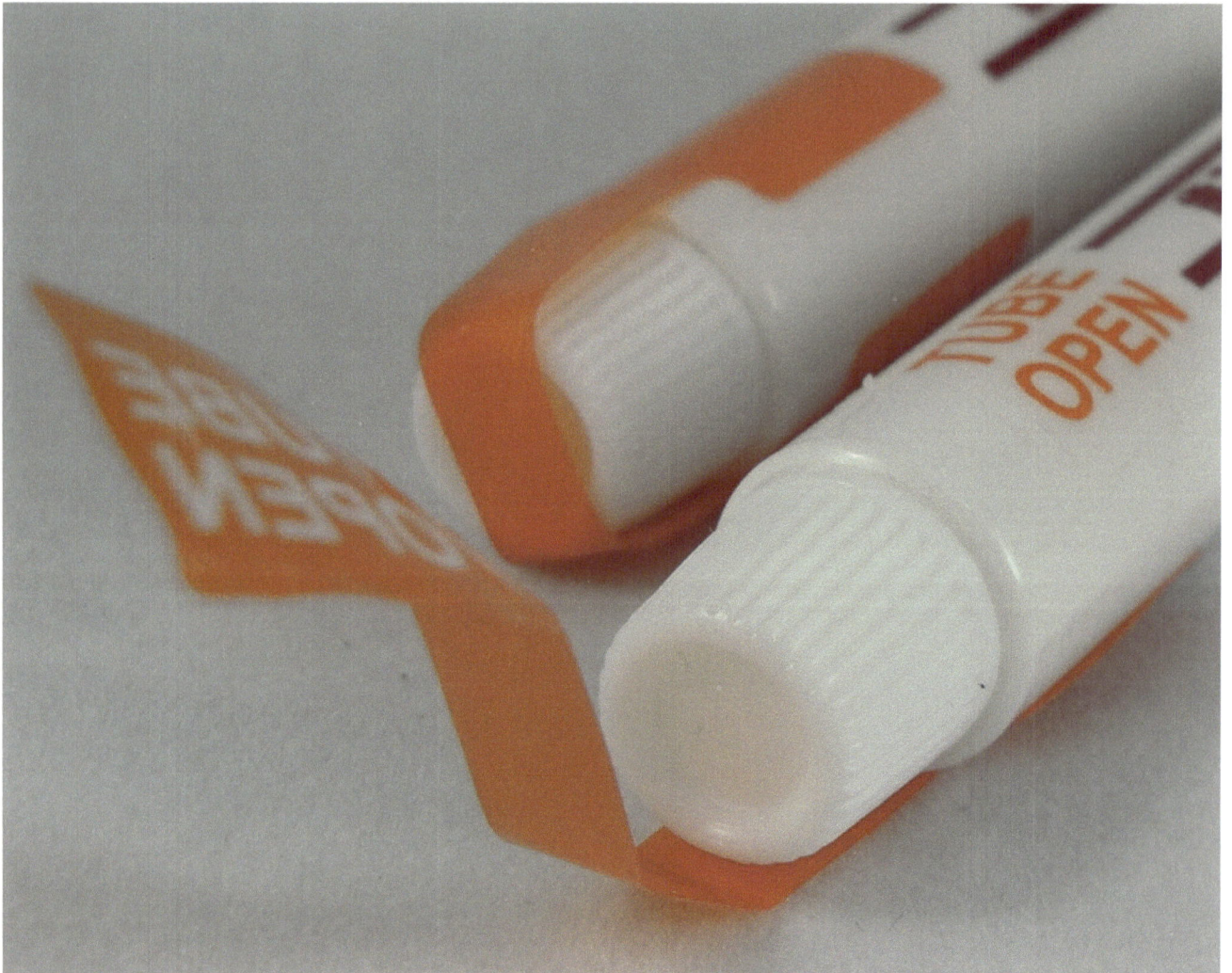

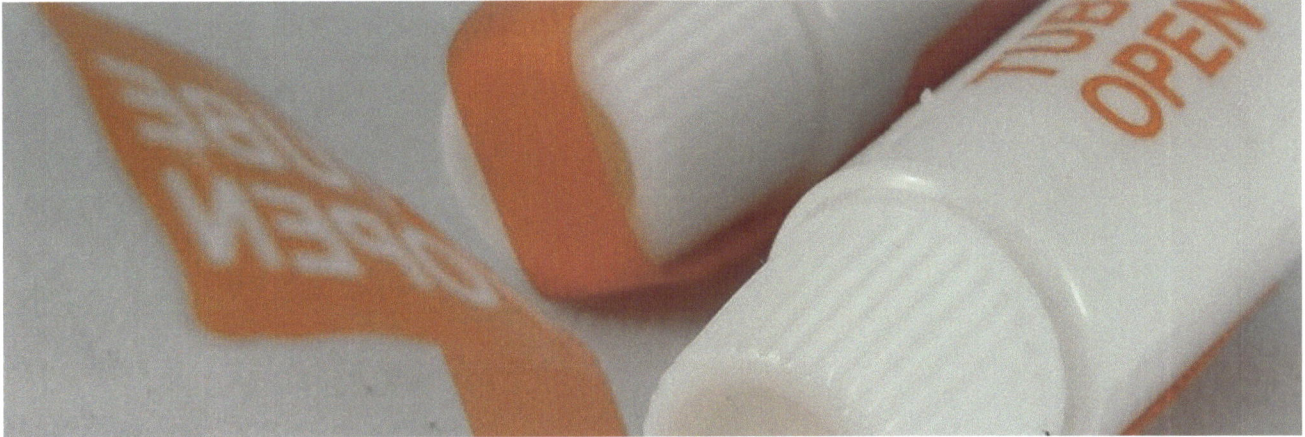

Manufacturer/Designer

Tamper Technologies Ltd,
The Oaks, Moor Farm Road West,
Airfield Industrial Estate, Ashbourne,
Derbyshire, DE6 1HD,
United Kingdom.
Phone: +44 (0) 1335 300335
Fax: +44 (0) 870 762 8968
Mobile: 07788 594 518
E-mail: chris@tampertech.com

• The tamper evident lable from TamperTech is a fast, flexible and inexpensive solution to secure products against theft and tampering.

• These innovative labels can be used as a marketing opportunity at the point of use by promoting a corporate message, validate product warranty, protect against counterfeiting and prove product authenticity.

• A tamper strip or label can be applied across the closure of a carton, lid of a bottle, seal of a container and a tamper tape can be used around shrink wrapped pallets and packaging boxes and these can include many unique features adding to your brand security as well as brand building through quality association.

• These security seals are available in standard colors, sizes and shapes but can be personalized with over printing of logos, bar codes, QR codes and sequential numbers.

• TamperTech labels can be applied to many different surfaces from glass, plastics and cardboard through to wood, painted metals and polythene bags, these labels and tapes are technical products with particular properties to suit different applications.

PHARMACEUTICAL PACKAGING INNOVATIONS

Manufacturer/Designer

Faubel & Co. Nachf. GmbH
Schwarzenberger Weg 45
34212 Melsungen Germany
Phone: +49 5661 7309-0
Fax: +49 5661 7309-149
Email: info@faubel.de

• Plus Label with index as an alternative to the multi layer Label and its many pages.

• Clear and "slim", this solution can easily replace conventional multi-layer label.

• It offers plenty of room for different language versions, warnings or instructions for use on 3 to 5 pages only.

• This is a way of ensuring higher patient safety and compliance, which comes particularly handy for our customers from the pharmaceutical industry.

• With their thumb indexes, both labeling solutions - the Faubel Compact®Label and the Plus Label - meet international market demands and give labeled products an obvious competitive advantage.

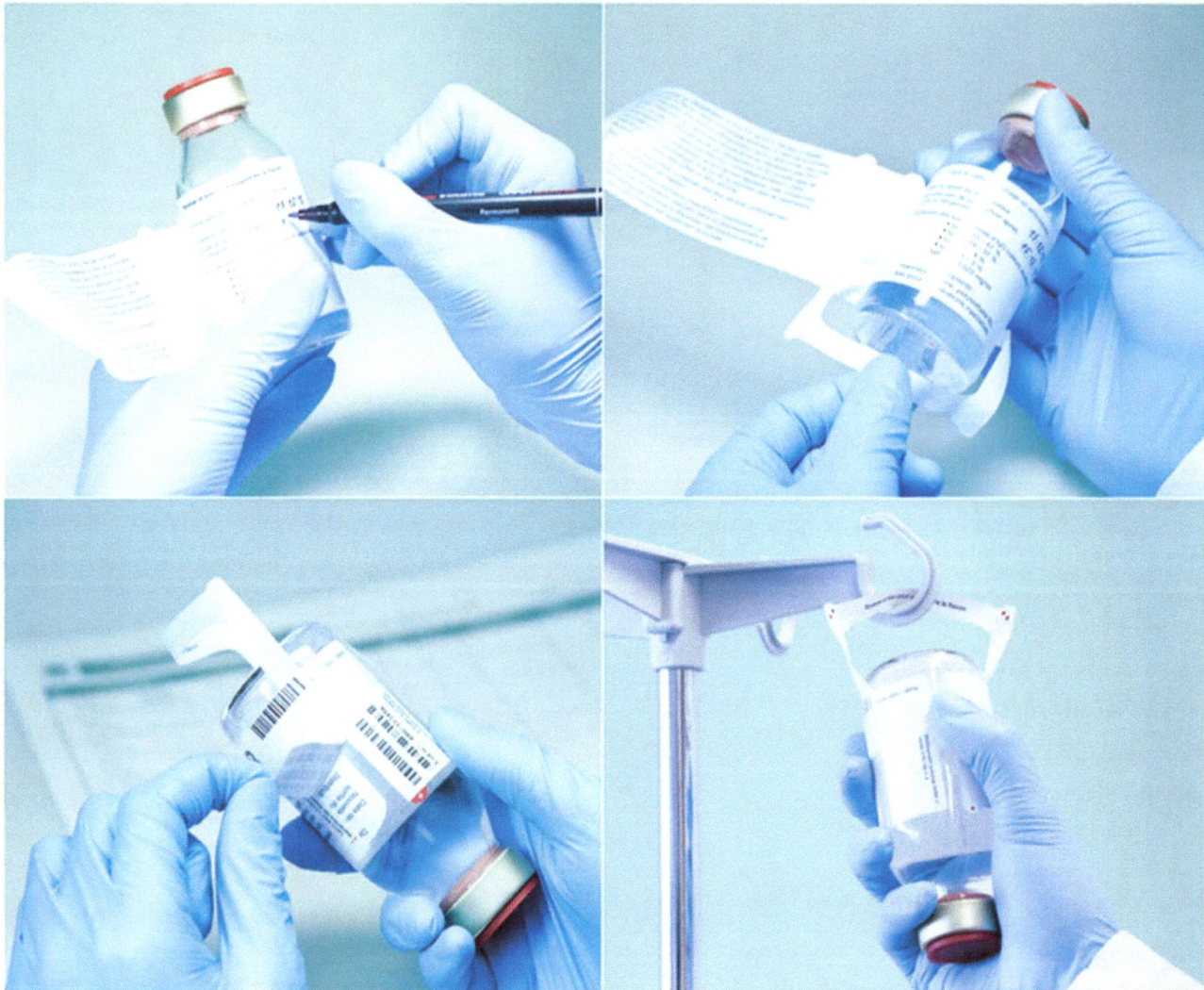

PHARMACEUTICAL PACKAGING INNOVATIONS

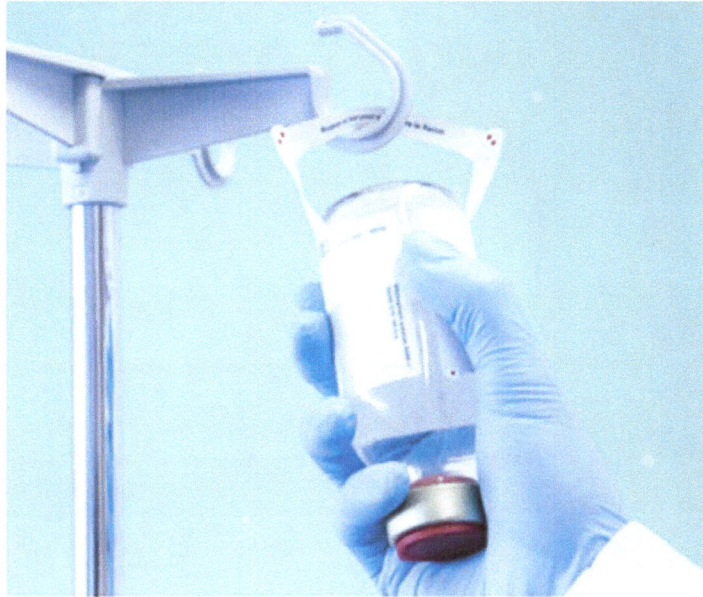

Manufacturer/Designer

SCHREINER GROUP GMBH & CO KG

BRUCKMANNRING 22

85764 OBERSCHLEIßHEIM, Germany

Tel: +49 89315840

Fax: +49 315845166

Email: info@schreiner-group.de

www.schreiner-group.com

• The Pharma-Tac Plus label combines product marking for infusion bottles with various integrated functions, including a booklet with sufficient space for extensive text in several languages, a secure and practical hanger, and detachable label parts for recording the medication.

• It is a sophisticated solution that adds value to the pharmaceutical manufacturer's end product and can be used in existing dispensing systems without any problems.

• It helps optimize processes carried out by medical staff and minimize medical errors.

•The Pharma-Tac Plus label allows end users to safely and efficiently hang infusion bottles.

• It also ensures that all important product information is readily available and facilitates recording of the administered medication.

PHARMACEUTICAL PACKAGING INNOVATIONS

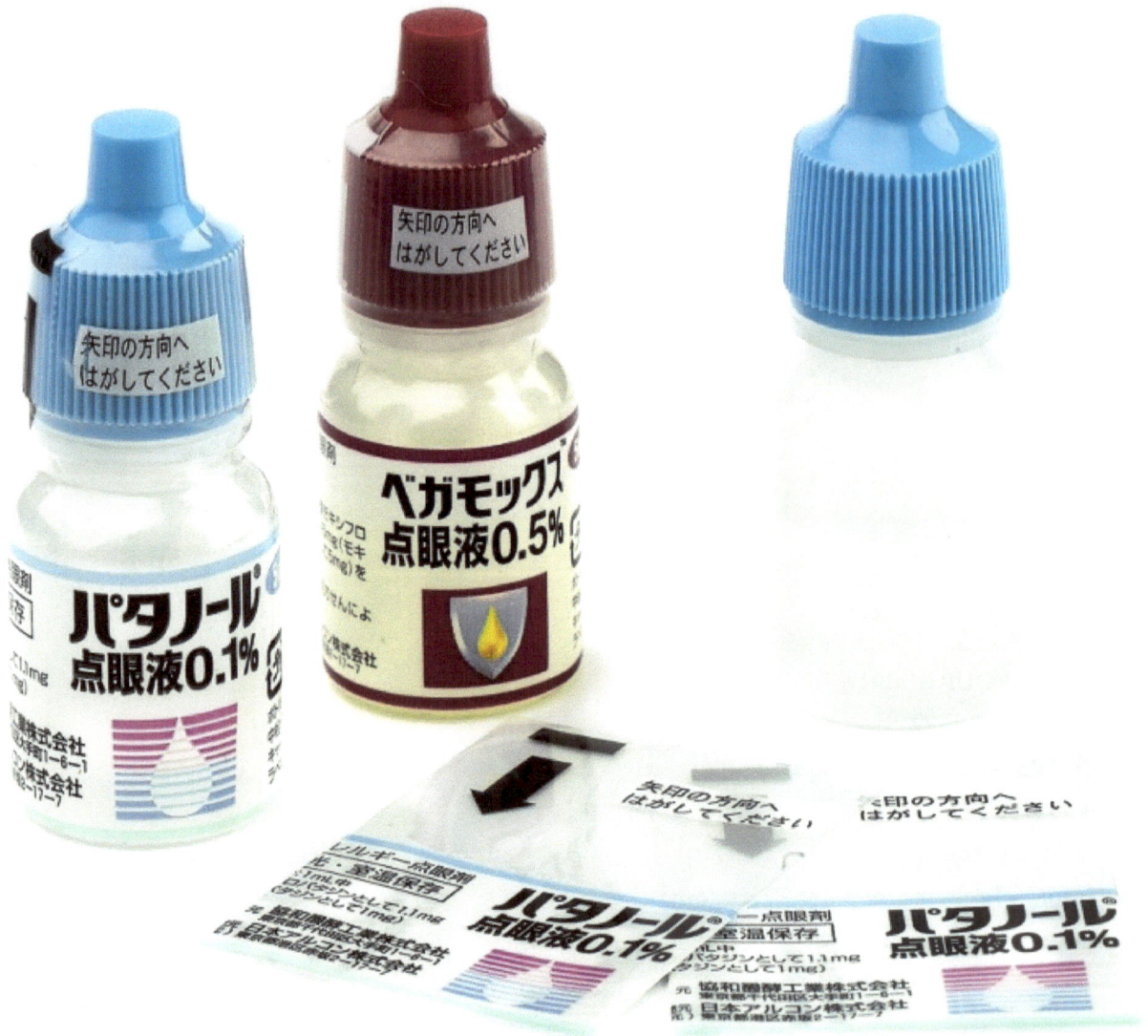

矢印の方向へ
はがしてください

ベガモックス
点眼液0.5%

パタノール
点眼液0.1%

パタノール
点眼液0.1%

パタノール
点眼液0.1%

矢印の方向へ
はがしてください

矢印の方向へ
はがしてください

PHARMACEUTICAL PACKAGING INNOVATIONS

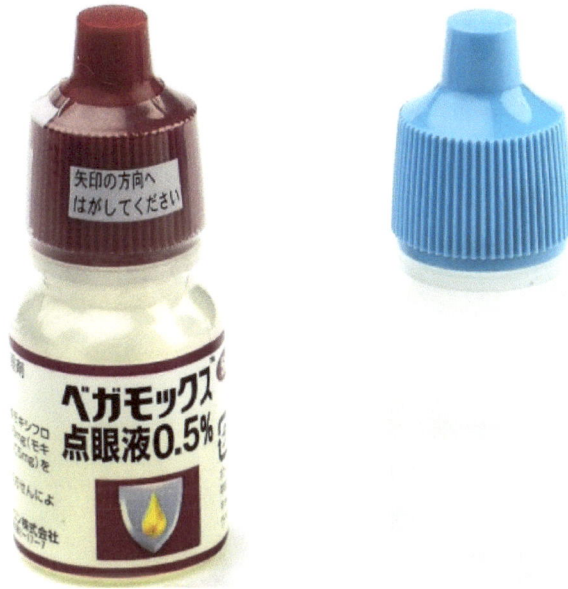

ベガモックス
点眼液0.5%

矢印の方向へ
はがしてください

Manufacturer/Designer

Sleever International® SA.
Aragon, 284 bis / 3° - 2 / 08007
Barcelona / Espana
Tel. 34 93 487 02 49
Fax. 34 93 487 28 58
sp.sleever@sleever.com
http://www.sleever.com/

• Sleever® packaging to protect, inform, meet regulatory requirements and fight against counterfeiting.
• A flexible answer to regulatory requirements: with the Sleever you can meet these printing evolutions with flexibility: Braille, Datamatrix, 9point text, leaflets and in the future serialization.
• All of these items are usually considered as a source of extra costs.
• These Lables are elements of satisfaction for marketing, the supply chain and user security.
• Labels correspond to the market's requirements and demands, and comply with the norms and regulations in force.

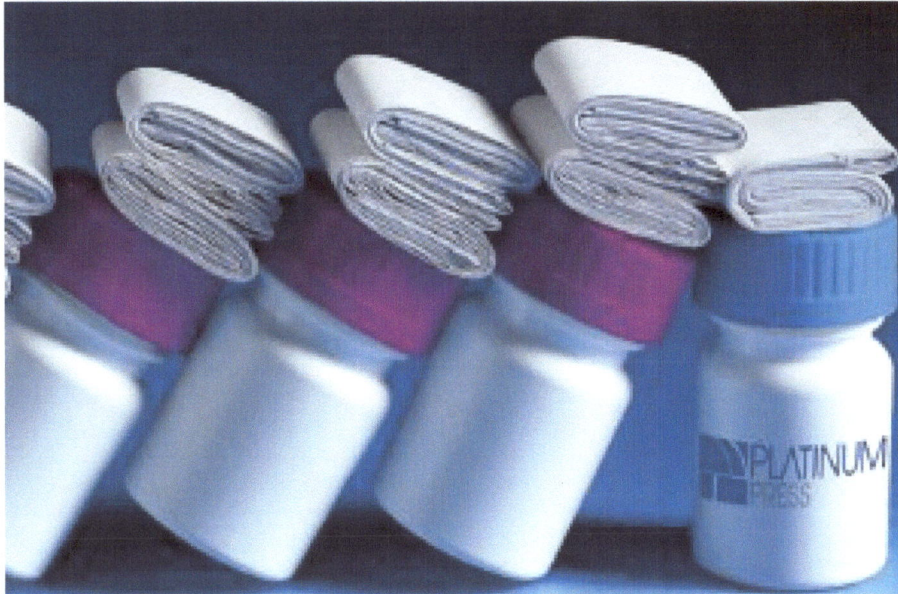

Manufacturer/Designer

Platinum Press
920 Avenue R
Building 200Grand
Prairie, TX 75050
Ph:469-733-1506
http://platinumpress.com

• New 266-Fold Outsert allows for an expanded number of panels which, in turn, yields a significant increase in copy space for necessary product information and instructions.

• As a result, the need for a "twinsert," or piggybacked outsert, often is eliminated.

• The 266-fold outsert is made possible through the company's advanced Vijuk MV-11 Knife System, which folds printed sheets as large as 21" X 40" into outserts as small as 1 1/8" X 1 1/8" (1.125" X 1.125") with as many as 266 panels.

• The result is a more compact printed component that increases production speeds and turnaround time while decreasing manufacturing costs.

• The 266-panel outserts are, on average, 20% thinner than traditional outserts, leading to a sleeker product appearance and customer savings on production, storage and shipping costs.

PHARMACEUTICAL PACKAGING INNOVATIONS

SECONDARY PACKAGING

EcoSavePack-frail pharmaceuticals

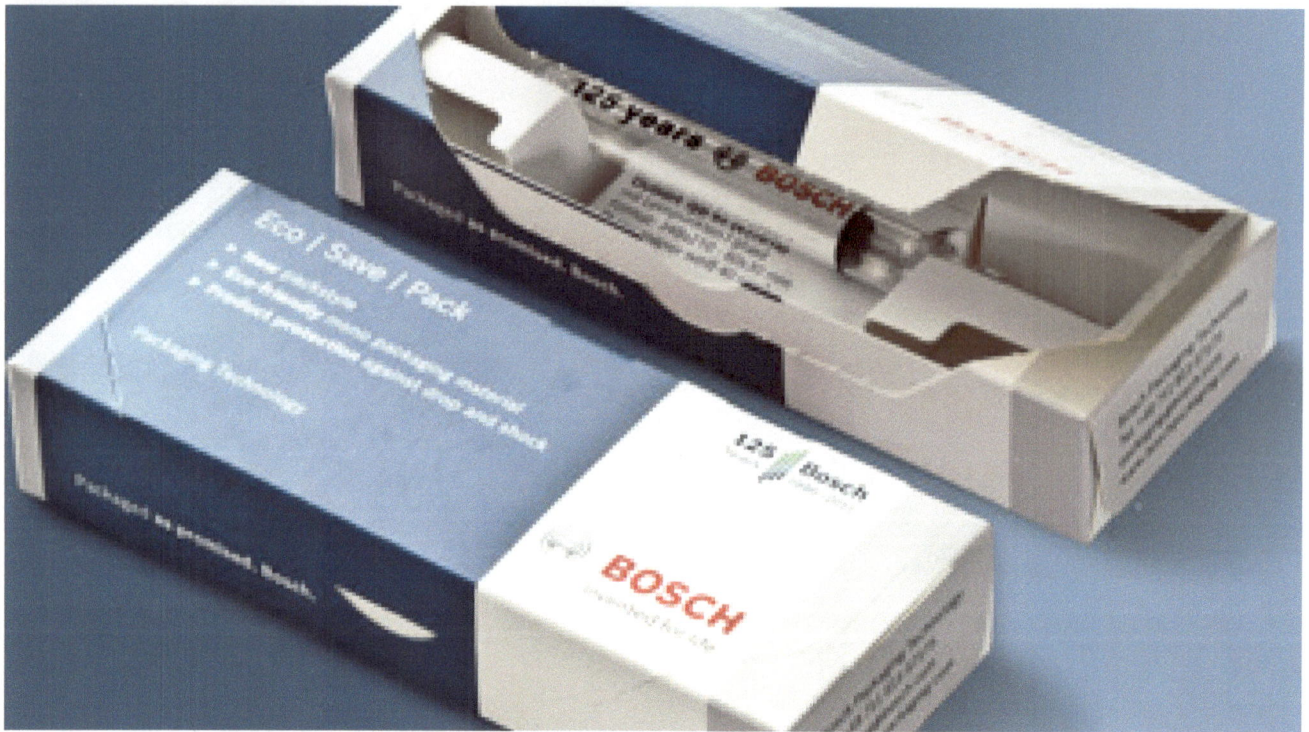

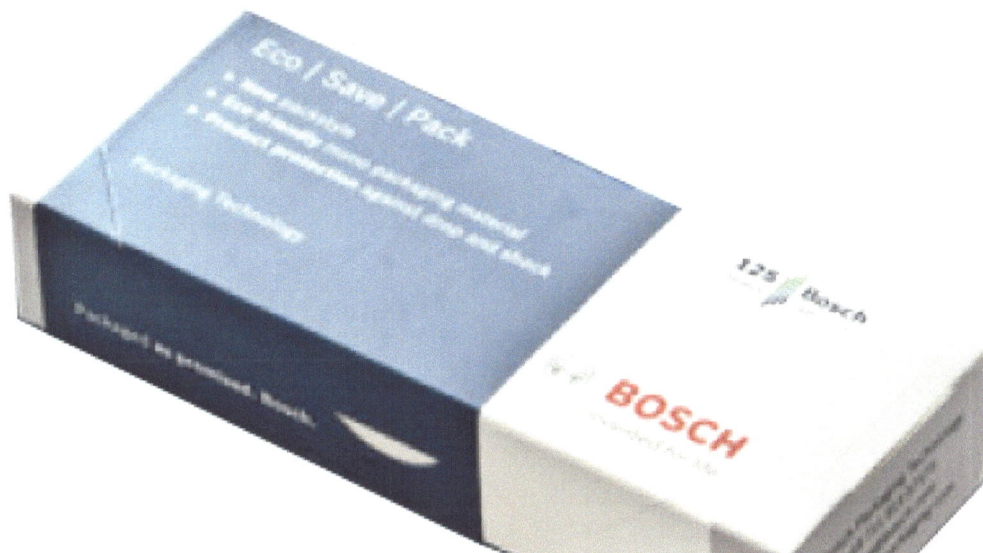

Manufacturer/Designer

Bosch Packaging Technology
Guenther Lade, Sales Manager
phone: +49 711 81157213
email: guenther.lade@bosch.com

• Many pharmaceutical products such as syringes, vials, ampoules or combination products require gentle handling to prevent transport damages.

• Bosch Packaging Technology and German folding cartons manufacturer August Faller KG have developed an innovative packaging style completely based on carton board.

• This offers the pharmaceutical industry sustainable secondary packaging system with the flexibility of handling various products and at the same time providing improved safety.

• Eco| Save| Pack is a carton tray with product-adapted inlays. Due to its chambered design, the inlays provide optimal protection. Inside the package the product is literally floating.

• It can be locked in place by clips, which prevents shifting and mutual contact.

• The reclosable, folded carton and the easy removal of the product from the inlay ensure a convenient handling of the packaging.

• The single packaging material makes the usage of a plastic tray and subsequently a thermoforming machine obsolete.

• Eco| Save| Pack is produced on the horizontal cartoning machine CUT 120.

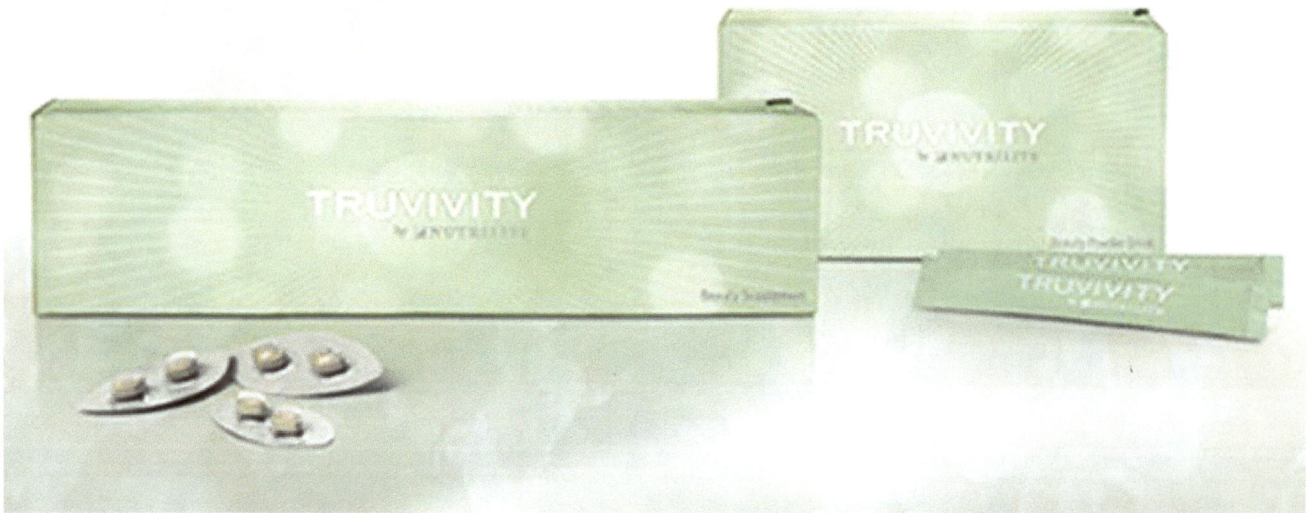

Manufacturer/Designer

TRUVIVITY by NUTRILITE
Telescoping Package
Amway Corporation

• An allegory to its brand promise 'Beauty From Within', telescoping packages bring unexpected luxury to a category ruled by underwhelming aesthetics.

• Proprietary design includes telescoping sleeve, reveal cover, tray with slotted insert and leaf-shaped blister packs.

• Innovative finishes like Liquid Soft Feel™, Liquid Lustre™ and Pearl Overlay add elegance and protection with efficient, one-pass printing.

• Global unification of components optimizes supply chain.

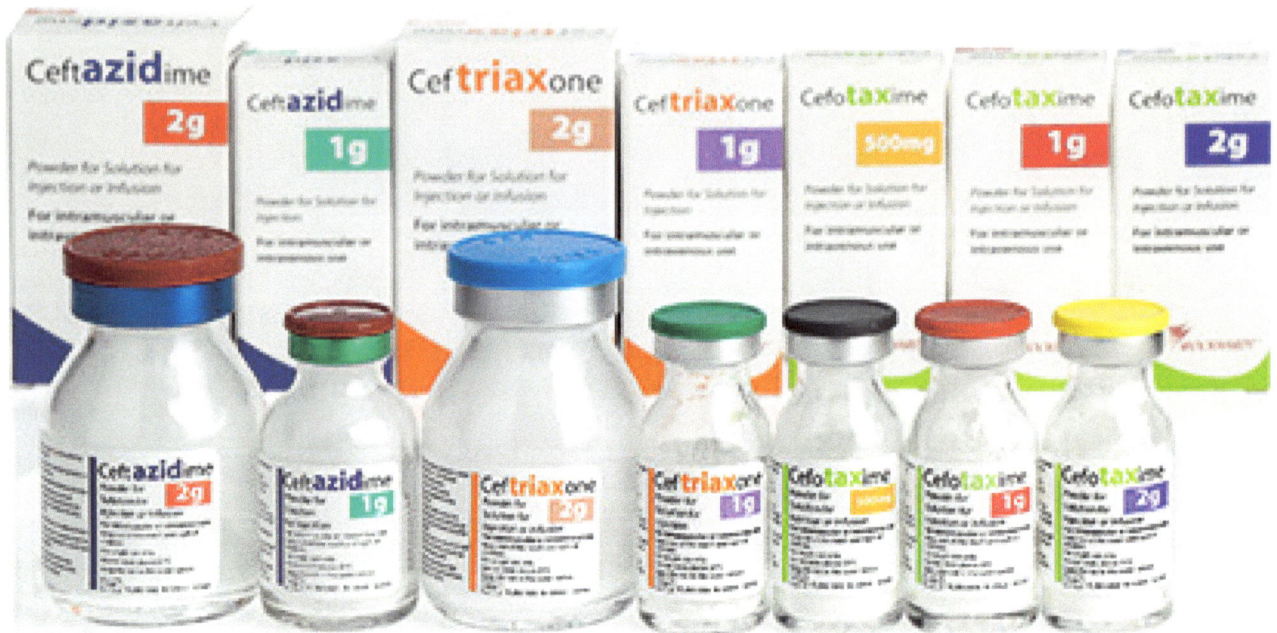

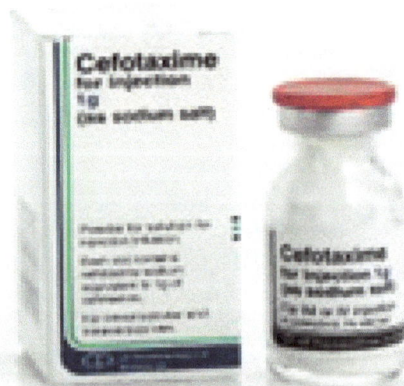

BEFORE

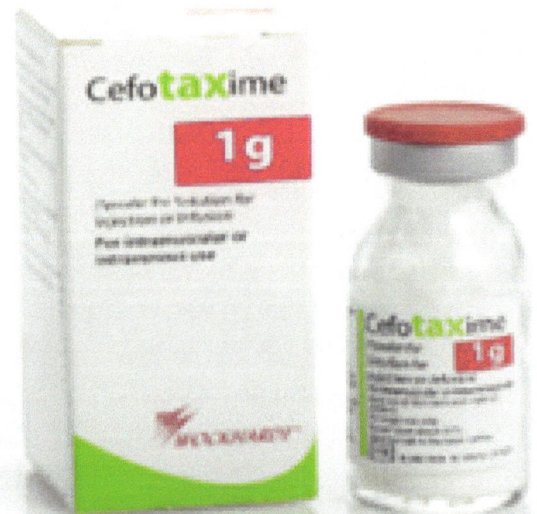

AFTER

PHARMACEUTICAL PACKAGING INNOVATIONS

Before
Cefotaxime

After
Cefo**tax**ime

Manufacturer/Designer

Wockhardt UK Limited

Ash Road North

Wrexham Industrial Estate Wrexham

LL13 9UF, U.K.

Tel: 01978 661261

Fax: 01978 660130

http://www.wockhardt.co.uk/

• A drive to improve patient safety is vitally important and packaging is playing its role.

• The key safety enhancements in this packaging include:

- Clearer font style and larger font sizes

- Carefully chosen colours to differentiate between product ranges and strengths, as recommended in the NPSA Guidelines.

- Route of administration (the way the medication is taken), clearly displayed on the front of the pack

- Duplication on the labels of the actual products where applicable.

• Popularly know as "Tall Man" lettering involves highlighting part of the drug's name on the packaging and also the labelling where applicable. For example, cefotaxime and ceftazidime are written as cefotaxime and ceftazidime, which helps to distinguish between look-alike and sound-alike product names, by clearly identifying and highlighting the different parts of the product names which may cause confusion.

• The aim of using Tall Man lettering is to reduce the risk of mis-selection.

• The MHRA have now issued guidance stating that the packaging and labelling for all generic cephalosporins - from all pharmaceutical companies should include the Tall Man lettering.

• Wockhardt UK was the first pharmaceutical company in the UK to use "Tall Man" lettering on packaging.

PHARMACEUTICAL PACKAGING INNOVATIONS

New Pharma Box For Ampoule

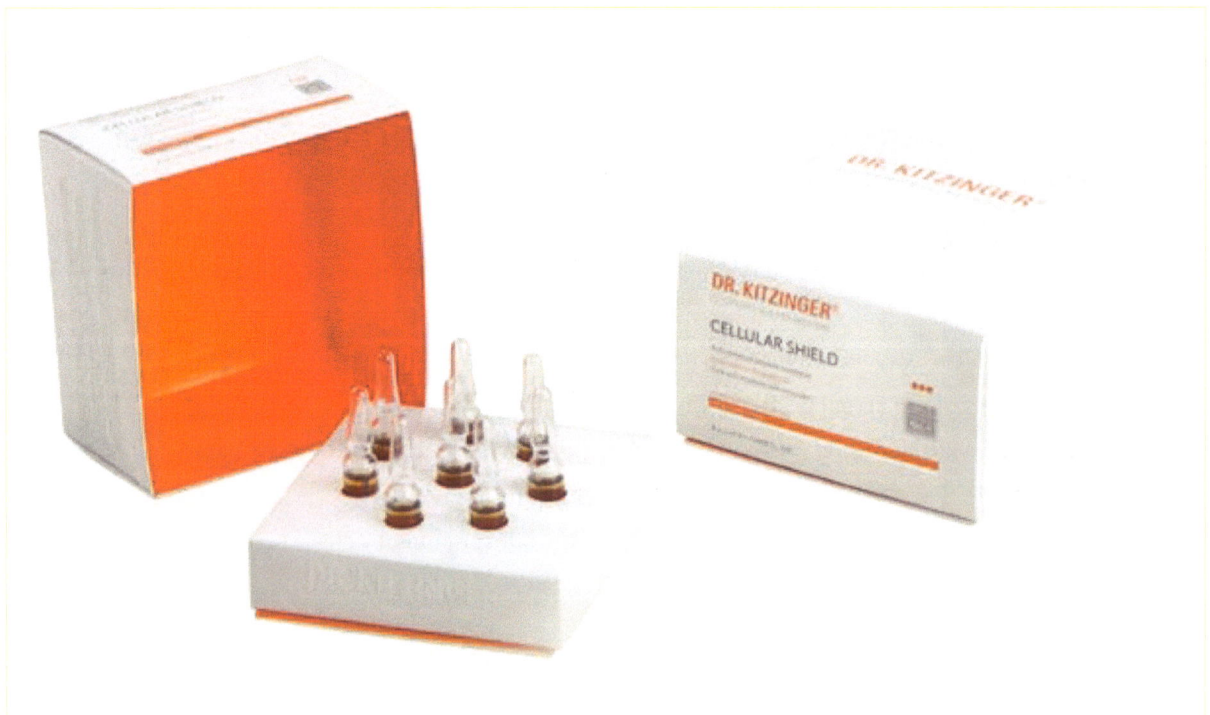

PHARMACEUTICAL PACKAGING INNOVATIONS

Manufacturer/Designer

STI Česko s.r.o.Zitna 123

CZ-40801 Rumburk

Tel: +420 412 354 800

Fax: +420 412 332 058

service.51@sti-group.com

http://www.sti-group.com/en/

- For the ampoule therapy the STI Group has developed a sophisticated cosmetics packaging with a premium finish and a special unpacking experience.
- The minimalist design elements in signal orange impart a clinical effect to the folding carton.
- The distinct whiteness of the box, silver foil embossing and reverse-side surface printing make for a perfect packaging finish.
- The bottom part is designed as a dual-chamber folding box in which the ampoules are placed vertically and so can be removed easily. Pre-glued edges on the lower part support the cover, preventing pressure on the ampoules during stacking.
- The overhanging edge of the packaging makes opening it effortless.

PHARMACEUTICAL PACKAGING INNOVATIONS

A Combined Carton and Insert

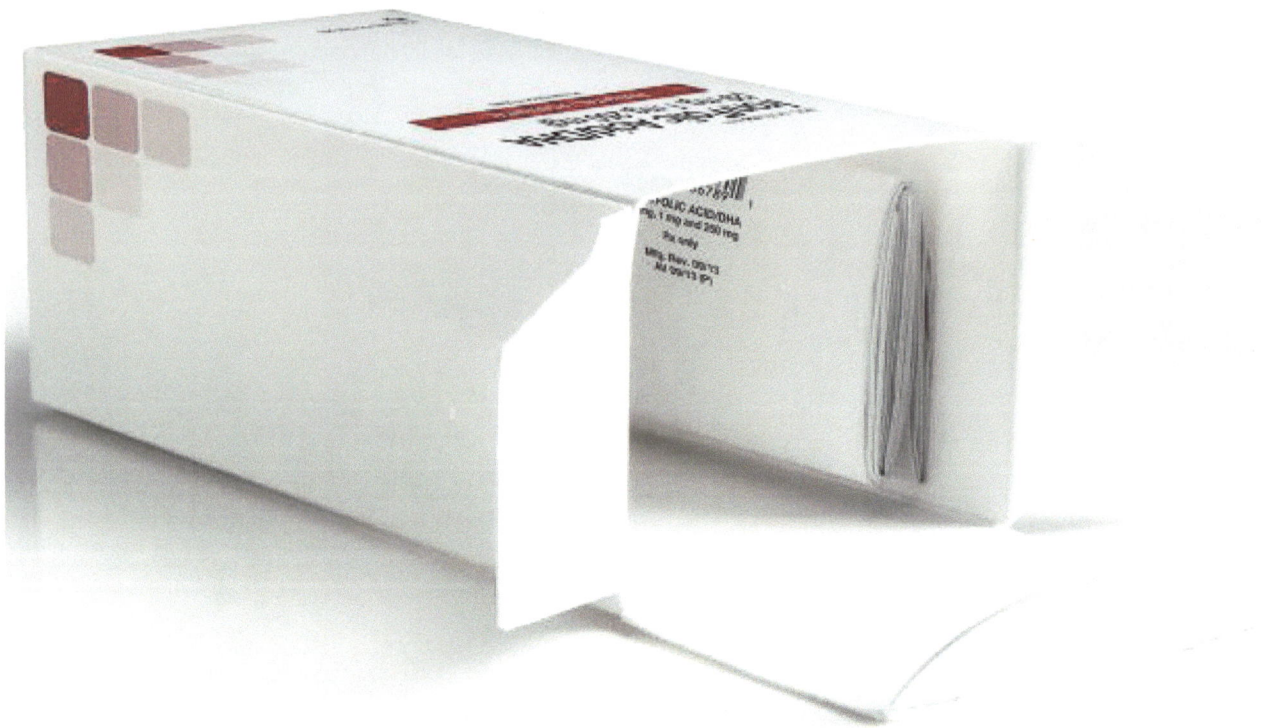

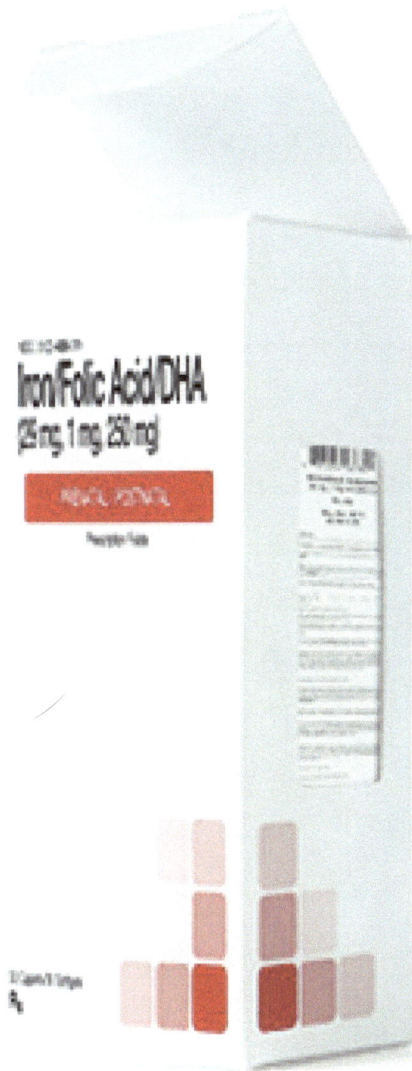

Manufacturer/Designer

Platinum Press
920 Avenue R
Building 200Grand
Prairie, TX 75050
Ph:469-733-1506
http://platinumpress.com/

• Platinum Press Inc. offers a combined carton and insert whereby the insert is consolidated into the carton itself.

• Option of Consolidating two or more printed components available to reduce complexity

• A window on each carton makes inserts visible for quality assurance inspection.

• Because fewer overall packaging components are needed, the carton/insert combo significantly reduces pack-out costs by increasing line speeds and diminishing machine downtime.

• The Combination Carton reduces cost, streamlines inventory and increases production.

• To guarantee a quality and accurate product, every insert and carton is electronically scanned and inspected to confirm a match.

PHARMACEUTICAL PACKAGING INNOVATIONS

Plastic Corrugated Returnable Package

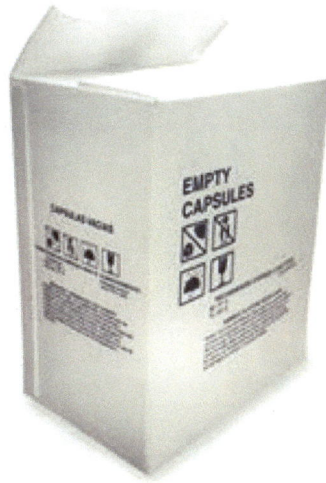

Manufacturer/Designer

AMTECH DESIGN COLUMBUS OH FACILITY
1633 Woodland Ave.
Columbus, OH 43219
Contact: 888-321-5445 ext 210
Email: info@amatechinc.com

• Plastic corrugated returnable packaging reduce packaging costs and provides better protection to products.

• Amatech is working with a number of pharmaceutical and medical companies to design returnable packaging for various products from vials and tubes to medicine and equipment.

• Setting a new standard for an industry that requires a high level of dependability and safety during shipping and storage.

• The company's 5-axis state of the art water jet cutter is capable of producing very intricate foam shapes and profiles to protect valuable parts and products.

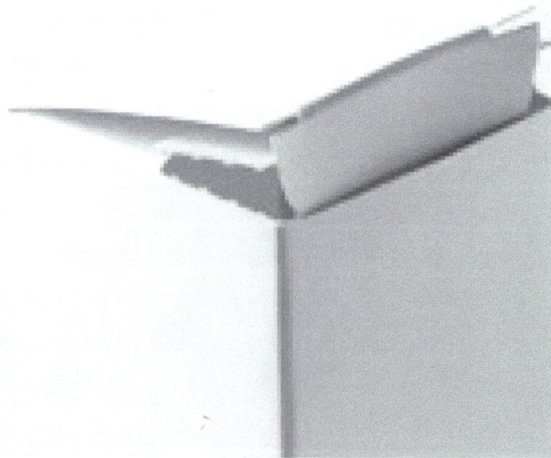

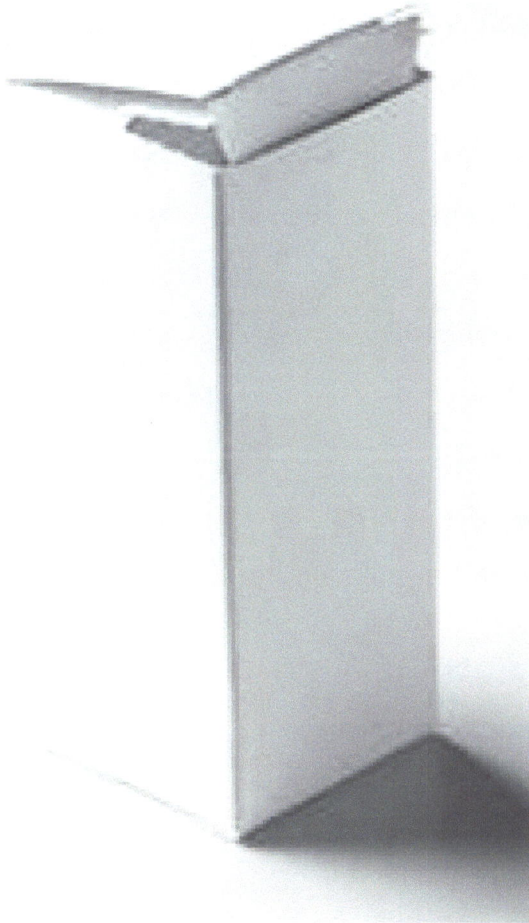

Manufacturer/Designer

August Faller KG
Freiburger Strasse 25
79183 Waldkirch Germany
Tel. +49 7681 405-196
Fax +49 7681 405-20196
Mob. +49 171 3049548
flora.herzog@august-faller.de
www.august-faller.de/

• Visible counterfeit features for which the authenticity is clearly recognisable for the patient are therefore a key focus of our development department. This includes, for example, folding cartons with engraved or perforated dust flaps.

• Easy way for pharmacists and patients to deal with medications.

• It is one of options for safe-guarding authenticity.

Features:

• Folding carton with tamper-evidence

• Counter-incisions or alternate perforations on the dust flap

• Targeted tearing when opening, through which tamper-evidence is clearly visible

• Machine processable

PHARMACEUTICAL PACKAGING INNOVATIONS

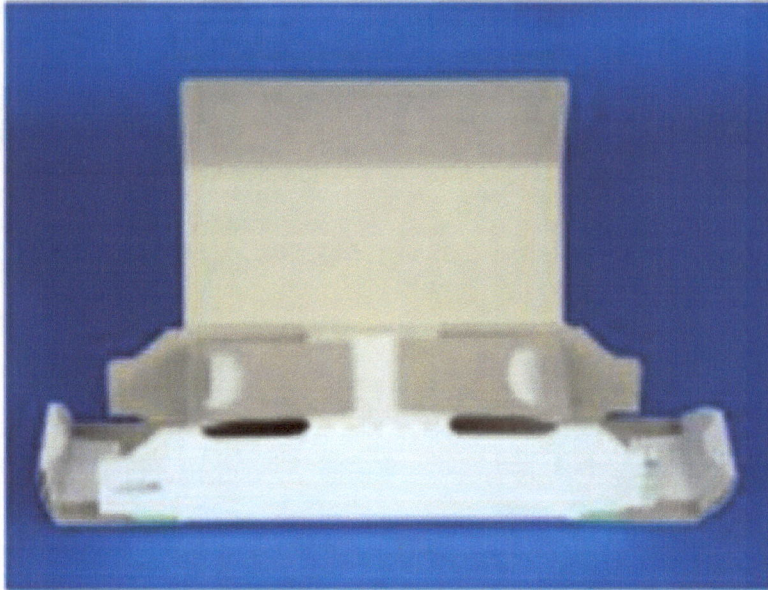

PHARMACEUTICAL PACKAGING INNOVATIONS

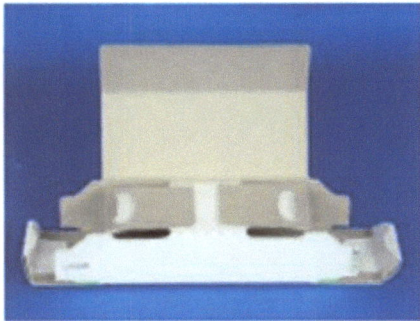

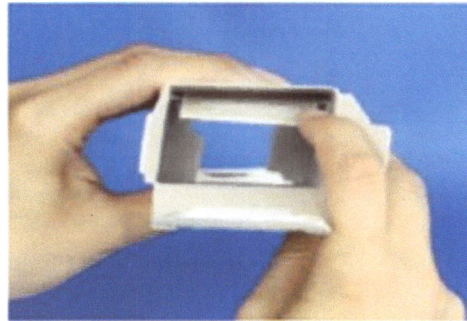

Manufacturer/Designer

Kyoshin Printing Co. Ltd.,

Japan

Yubinbango154-0023

Setagaya-ku, Tokyo

Wakabayashi 4-39-1

TEL: 03-5433-2802 Fax: 03 3412-6204

yuinagawa@kyoshin-pr.co.jp

www.kyoshin-pr.co.jp

• The concept of this package is to assure the effectiveness of the packaging of medical products.

• It is equipped with a double-locking security mechanism to prevent the breaking of the seal by unauthorized people, or theft of the product.

• Additionally, this package is made from 100% paper and its design allows it to be manufactured on the existing automated package line, significantly cutting down on waste.

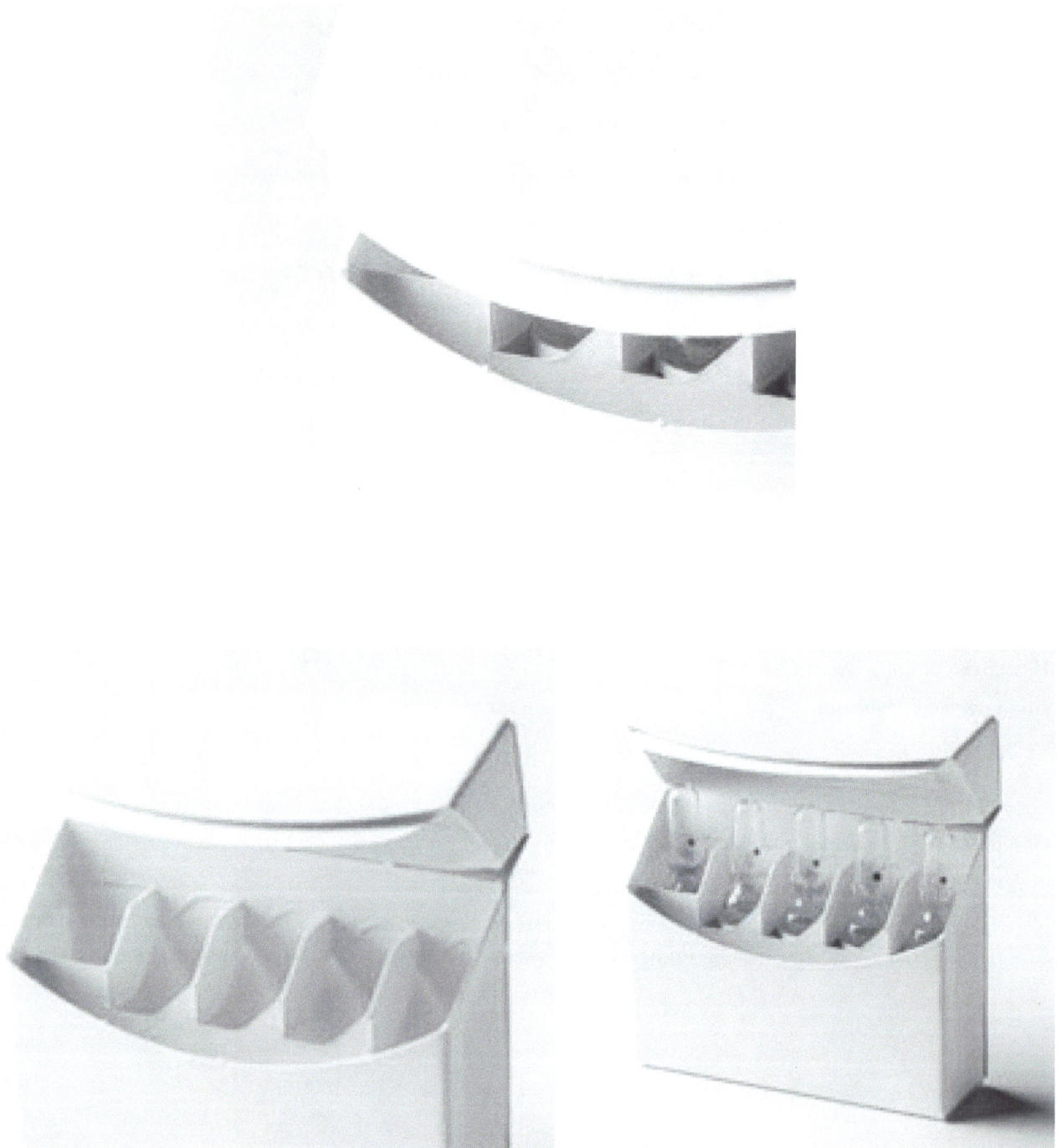

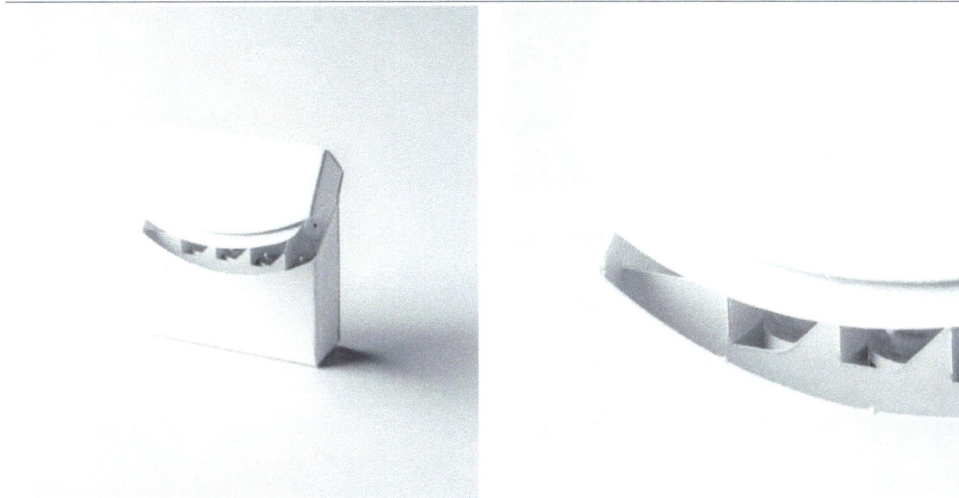

Manufacturer/Designer

August Faller KG

Freiburger Strasse 25

79183 Waldkirch Germany

Tel. +49 7681 405-196

Fax +49 7681 405-20196

Mob. +49 171 3049548

flora.herzog@august-faller.de

www.august-faller.de/

• Easy-to-open Folding Carton With Internal Compartment is a compliance & Convenience packaging .

• Easy-to-open folding carton constructions is with internal compartment.

Features

•Easy opening through extra large plug-in flap

• Product independence

• Tamper-evident closure

• Machine processablilty

PHARMACEUTICAL PACKAGING INNOVATIONS

MACHINES

PHARMACEUTICAL PACKAGING INNOVATIONS

Manufacturer/Designer

MG2 S.r.l.
Via del Savena 18,
40065 Pian di Macina di Pianoro,
Bologna, Italy
Tel: +39 051 4694111
Fax: +39 051 4694199
Email: sales@mg2.it

• FlexaLAB for containment is a capsule filler for laboratories.

• The containment system features a particular liftable isolator concept, which allows the machine to keep its peculiarity to change different dosing units.

• This result is obtained while ensuring proper production safety, for both the operator and the environment; in fact, the system allows the machine to satisfy the highest containment class, OEL5, guaranteeing a concentration of active substance lower than 1 μg per cubic metre.

• FlexaLAB containment version can be equipped with a Wet-in-Place system, which allows to fix powders when the production cycle ends, before opening the isolator.

• Through the same spray gun it is possible to use both liquids and compressed air. By adding some spray balls and other devices, FlexaLAB is configured for a complete Wash-In-Place system, to further automate the cleaning process.

• Other optional devices enable to customize the production outfeed to an external container or a continuous liner, as well as the connection to other devices, such as a deduster or a metal detector.

PHARMACEUTICAL PACKAGING INNOVATIONS

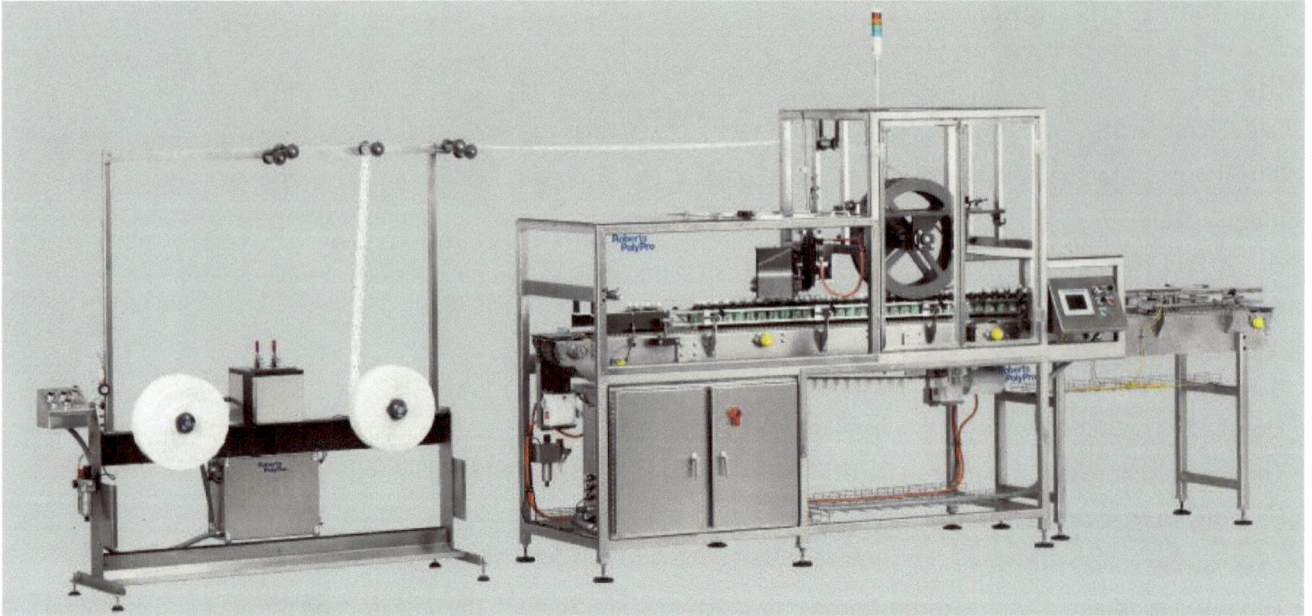

HDPE
All handles are
100% recyclable

All handles can
be supplied in
any PMS color

Manufacturer/Designer

Roberts PolyPro, Inc.
5416 Wyoming Avenue Charlotte,
NC 28273 United States
Tel.: 1-800-269-7409
Phone: 704-588-1794
Fax: 704-588-1821
www.robertspolypro.com
info@robertspolypro.com

• This new up to 600 bottles-per-minute handle applicator utilizes a continuous motion roll-feed design to achieve 2, 4, 6, 8, and 12 packs.

• The handle applicator utilizes a continuous motion roll-feed design that reduces the cost of handle dies as well as the number of dies required: one die/bottle neck size, not pack-size configuration.

• The latest generation of fully-recyclable HDPE handles are thin, light, and strong. The cost compared to the previous generation of handles has fallen by 26% principally from a 28% reduction in material sourced/handle.

• Operators no longer have to fill stacks of handles into a machine magazine, but simply load a roll of handles onto the machine. To change rolls, operators weld the end of the in-use roll to the beginning of the next roll with one push of a button. Each machine accommodates two rolls of handles. These features help reduce labor costs.

• In the past, handles were applied at the end of the packaging line to bottles already packed in cases. This limited throughput to fewer than 500 bottles/min. The new machine is located right after the capper, reducing the footprint of the new machine.

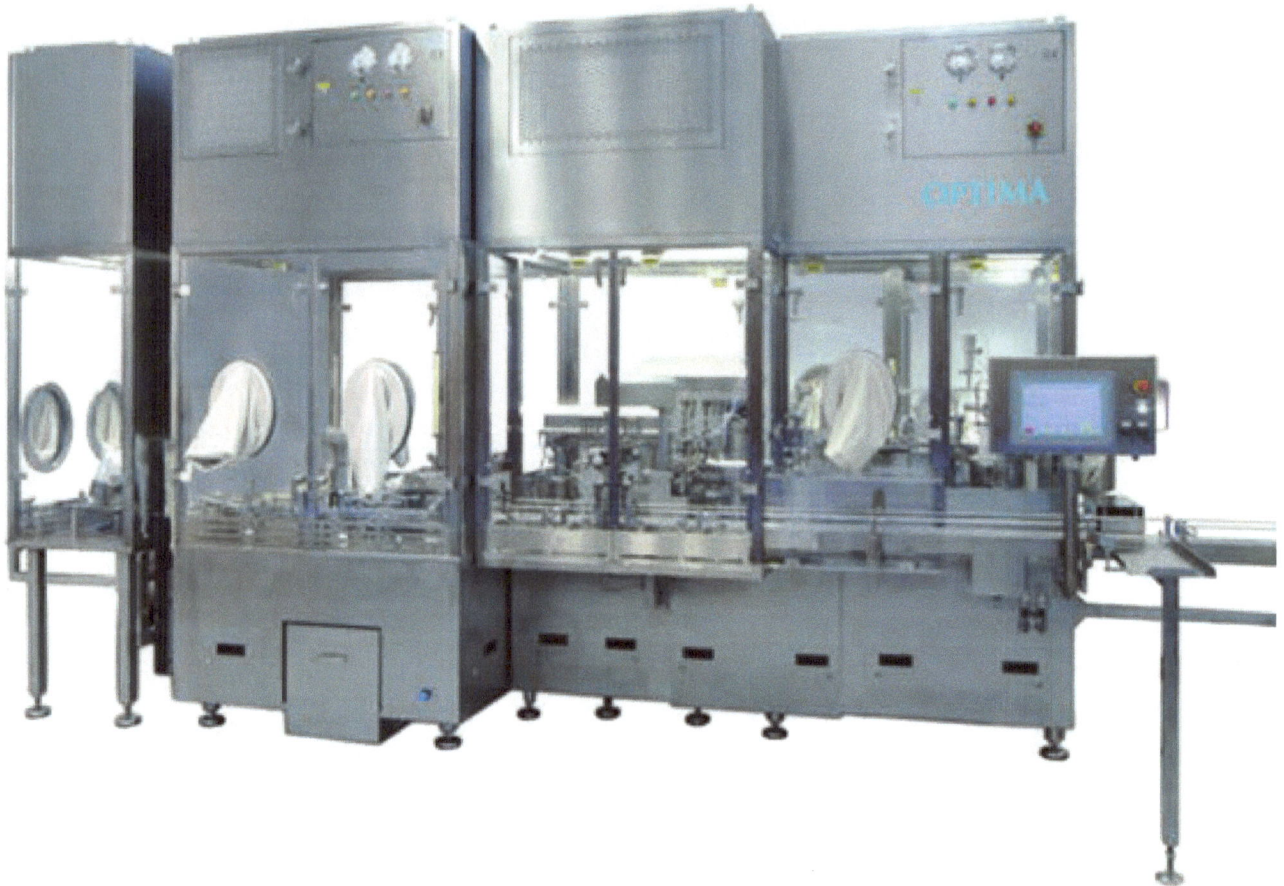

Manufacturer/Designer

OPTIMA packaging group GmbH
Steinbeisweg 20
74523 Schwäbisch Hall, Germany
Postfach 10 05
2074505 Schwäbisch Hall, Germany
Phone: +49 791 506-0
Fax: +49 791 506-9000
http://www.optima-group.de
info@optima-group.de

• The INOVA SV125, a modular filling and closing machine is suitable for pilot testing to outputting medium volumes up to 18,000 containers/hour achieved via ten filling points.

• Optima's upgraded Inova SV125modular filling and closing machine has a dosing range of 0.1 to 50 ml.

• The system flexibility is such that the operator can implement up to three difference filling systems in a single machine while also processing three different container types: nested syringes, carpules and vials.

• Additional modules and functions can be integrated, including filling under vacuum, pre- and post-flushing with gas and up to 100% in-process control.

• Upstream, the pre-sterilised containers are manually to fully automatically unpacked and fed to the process.

• The post-processing section features such modules as backstop locks and safety devices, optical and sensor controls, labellers and track and trace systems. RAB systems and isolators can be deployed for containment.

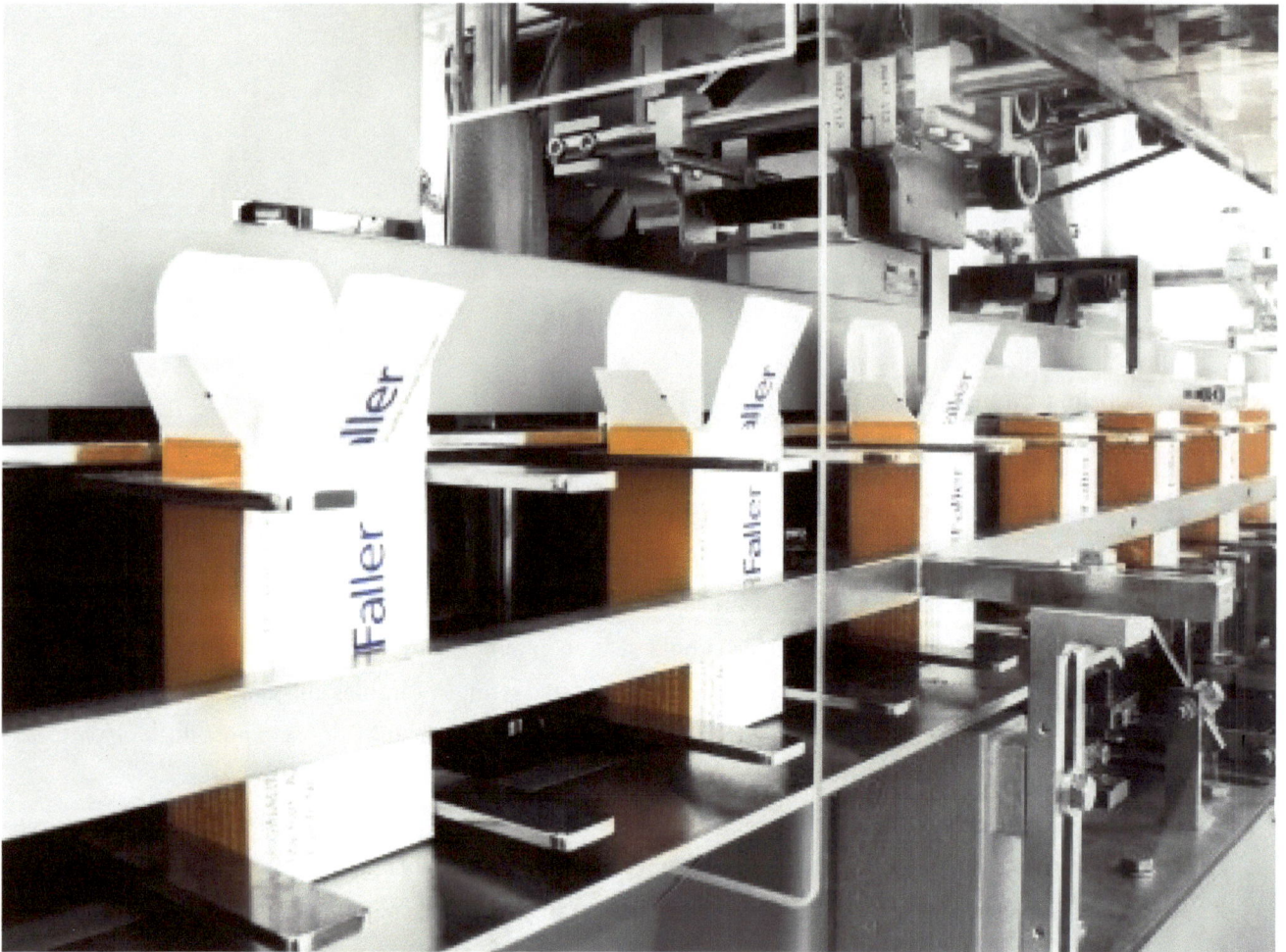

PHARMACEUTICAL PACKAGING INNOVATIONS

Manufacturer/Designer

AUGUST FALLER KG
FREIBURGER STRAßE 25,
79183 WALDKIRCH, Germany
Tel: +49 76814050
Fax: +49 7681405110
Email: info@august-faller.de
www.august-faller.de/

• August Faller KG's new Faller 1209 is a fast and efficient packaging of ampoules, vials and pens using a customised automated solution for small and medium runs.

• In addition to accelerating the entire filling process, the new solution also provides a maximum process speed and thus allows a shorter time-to-market.

• Providing high degree of flexibility, especially when it comes to small and medium batch sizes.

• It improve overall equipment effectiveness as well as a short time-to-market.

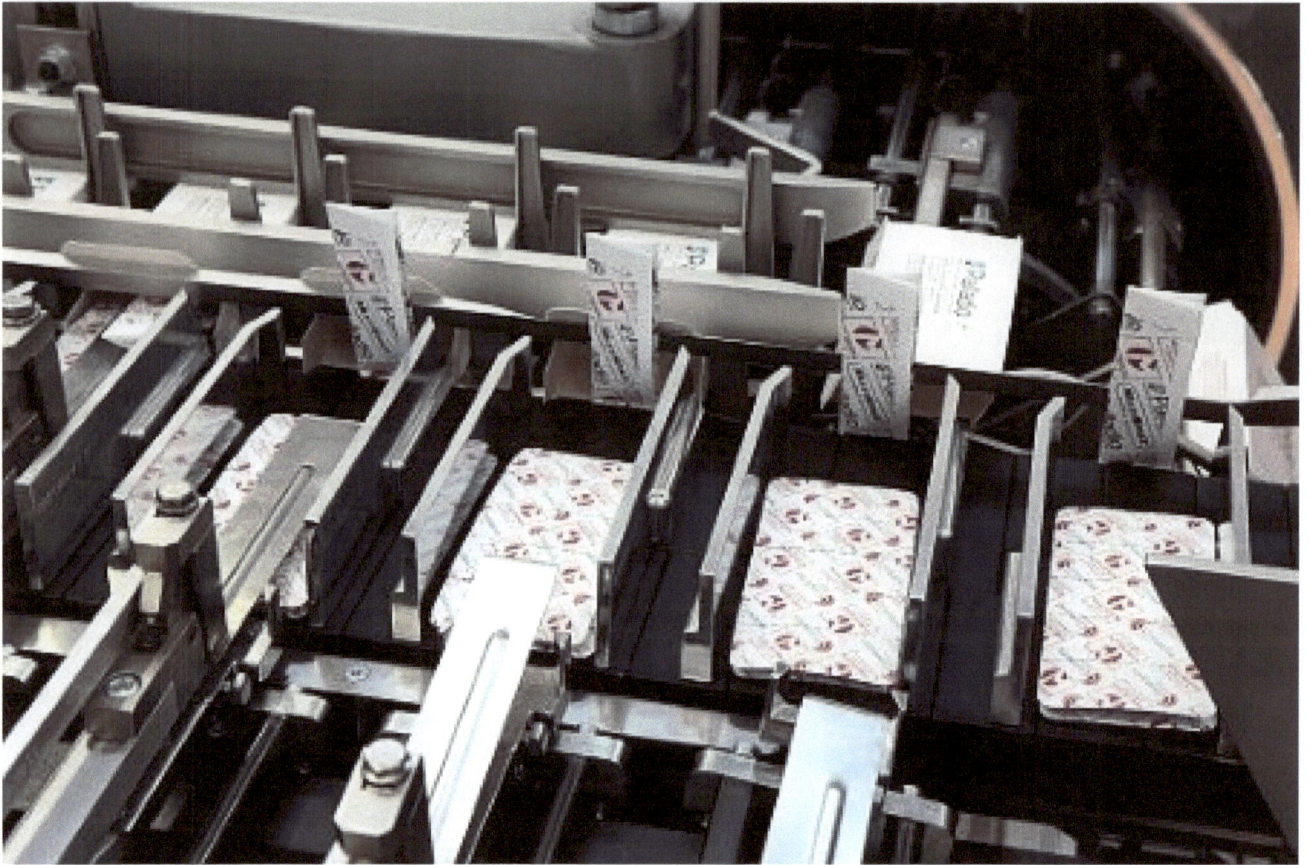

PHARMACEUTICAL PACKAGING INNOVATIONS

Manufacturer/Designer

MARCHESINI, SRL
VIA PIEMONTE 24 - FRAZ. OSTERIA GRANDE,
40060 CASTELSAN PIETRO TERME (BO), Italy
Tel: +39 051945422
Fax: +39 051945428
Email: marchesini@alinet.it

• The packaging line) is a highly-innovative, fully automated line able to handle up over 300 prefilled syringes in a minute.

• The line is composed by the thermoformer FBZ 320 and the continuous motion cartoner BA 400 Argento and is specifically designed for the syringe packaging market..

• FBZ 320 is a mechanical intermittent motion fully automatic packaging machine that thermoforms trays for vials, ampoules, syringes and similar products out of thermoformable films such as PVC and PET.

• The quality of the finishes, the extreme sturdiness and the tool-less size change-over make this machine highly reliable, flexible and user-friendly.

• ZERO-WASTE version with high-speed die-cutter, a feature that increases speed and performance and reduces rejects.

• FBZ 320 with BA 400 Argento, the high speed horizontal continuous motion cartoner that can handle up to 360 cartons in a minute. It combines the advantages of reduced overall dimensions with greater sturdiness and improved reliability.

• This cartoner, due to the balcony layout, has a completely enclosed structure with safety devices on all the opening parts to ensure overall protection and compliance with all the current safety regulations.

PHARMACEUTICAL PACKAGING INNOVATIONS

PHARMACEUTICAL PACKAGING INNOVATIONS

Manufacturer/Designer

Olmec Ltd
Unit 4, Falkland Way, Barton-Upon-Humber,
North Lincolnshire, DN18 5RL, United Kingdom
Tel: 44 (0)1652 631960
Email: info@olmec-uk.com

• Olmec UK has designed and manufactured a line scan-based vision system for 100% inspection of labels on OTC healthcare product bottles.

• By rotating the bottle in front of the camera, the label is effectively 'unwrapped' to produce an image equivalent to imaging before it was stuck to the bottle.

• The vision system checks that the information on the label is correct as well as identifying missing or partial print.

• The system handles a variety of bottles at a variety of speeds. The bottles are randomly fed into a servo-controlled starwheel which rotates each bottle in turn to the camera position.

• The 'unwrap' process is achieved by using rollers to then rotate the bottle within the pocket of the starwheel in front of a line scan camera which builds up the image of the label line by line.

• A distortion-free image is produced so there are no false rejects and no possibility of any rogue products getting through.

The Travtec Aggregation

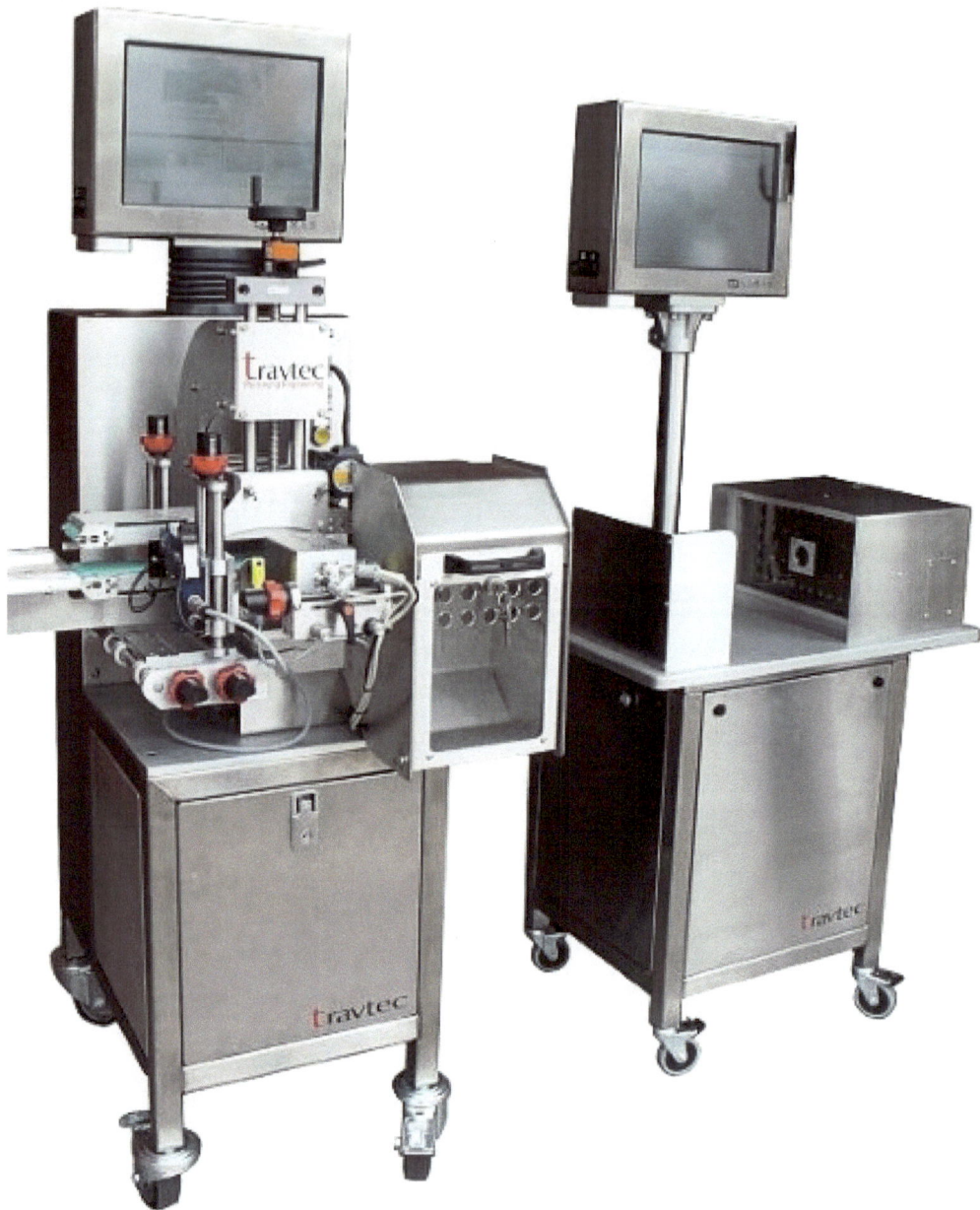

Manufacturer/Designer

TRAVTEC LFtrTD
11 COMMONWEALTH CLOSE,
LEIGH BUSINESS PARK,LEIGH,
WN7 3BD, United Kingdom
Tel: +44 1942677664
Fax: +44 1942261101
Email: info@travtec.uk.com
http://www.travtec.co.uk/

• The Travtec Aggregation is a new traceability module.

• The Travtec Aggregation Module allows any pack to be traced from its manufacture to the end-user, which means that companies will now be able to future-proof against further traceability legislation.

• It is increasingly being specified by other regulatory bodies for other markets, according to Travtec.

• The software can also be incorporated into Travtec's Pharmacarton carton handling, marking and verifying system to enable a unique label to be prepared at each stage of the packing operation.

Manufacturer/Designer

Robert Bosch GmbH

Bosch Service Center Postfach 30 02

2070442 StuttgartGERMANY

Tel: 49 (0)711 400 40990

Fax:+49 (0)711 400 40999

http://www.bosch.com/en/

• New Sigpack HCUL horizontal flow wrapper for packaging individual vials with a capacity to package up to 300 single blow-fill-seal (BFS) vials per minute.

• The machine uses long-dwell cross-sealing technology that ensures hermetic packages even at high speed.

• The balcony design of the cross-sealing unit with individually mounted heating elements allows for easy access and fast changeover.

• It can be equipped with either ultrasonic or heat sealing technology, as per the application

• This system has primary packaging units, delivered as BFS cards, which are inserted into the machine with the help of a Sigpack LDF Delta robot or other intelligent loading solutions.

• Sigpack HCUL flow wrapper, with a control system, has the capability of monitoring the alignment of the products, as well as the information printed on the packaging, such as the barcode.

• The machine will deliver only hermetically sealed packages while the packages that are not compliant with the specifications are automatically rejected.

• It can accommodate modified atmosphere packaging (MAP) and can be modified for a variety of functions, such as the innovative real-time MAP system.

• The RT-MAP and the sensor for measuring residual oxygen content are integrated in the sealing unit, which enables real-time measurement of residual oxygen content in the package, rejecting those that have excessive residual oxygen.

DISCLAIMER

• This presentation by PackagingConnections (PC) contains information that are provided is accurate to best of our knowledge

• The information provided by the PC in this presentation is general in nature and is not intended as a guide to individual concerns.

• Unauthorized attempts to modify any information stored on this presentation or to use them for any purposes other than its intended purposes are prohibited.

• PackagingConnections makes no warranties, guarantees, or representations as to the accuracy of information contained in this presentation, and assumes no liability or responsibility for any errors in the content.

• Certain names and logos are trademarks and service marks of PackagingConnections and its clients may not be used without permission. Product names, logos, brands, and other trademarks featured or referred to within the presentation are the property of their respective trademark holders.

PHARMACEUTICAL PACKAGING INNOVATIONS

Dear Readers!
Thank you for your interest.

We are capable of providing customized reports and surveys.
For further details contact:

amita.venkatesh@packagingconnections.com

CONTACT US

CORPORATE OFFICE

Sanex Packaging Connections Pvt. Ltd.
(ISO 9001:2008 certified company)
117, Suncity Business Tower
Golf course road, Sector--54
Gurgaon-122002
India
Tel: +91 124 4965770
Fax: +91 124 4143951

Email: info@packagingconnections.com
Website:www.PackagingConnections.com